HERE COME THE BLACK HELICOPTERS!

HERE COME THE BLACK HELICOPTERS!

UN Global Governance and the Loss of Freedom

DICK MORRIS
and EILEEN McGANN

BROADSIDE BOOKS
An Imprint of HarperCollins*Publishers*
www.broadsidebooks.net

HarperCollins books may be purchased for educational, business, or sales promotional use. For information, please e-mail the Special Markets Department at SPsales@harpercollins.com.

Broadside Books™ and the Broadside logo are trademarks of HarperCollins Publishers.

FIRST EDITION

Library of Congress Cataloging-in-Publication Data has been applied for.

ISBN: 978-0-06-224059-0

12   13   14   15   16   DIX/RRD   10 9 8 7 6 5 4 3 2 1

To our Founding Fathers.
Let us preserve the great nation they built.

WARNING: READING THIS BOOK AND ADOPTING ITS PREMISE MAY BE DANGEROUS TO YOUR REPUTATION AND LEAD TO CRITICISM AND RIDICULE FROM LIBERALS, GLOBALISTS, AND RADICAL ENVIRONMENTALISTS.

BUT, UNDERSTAND THIS: IF THEY HAVE THEIR WAY, THE AMERICA WE KNOW AND LOVE WILL NO LONGER EXIST.

BECAUSE THEIR PLANS FOR GLOBAL GOVERNANCE—THROUGH THE UNITED NATIONS AND ITS RELATED AGENCIES—ARE AT SERIOUS ODDS WITH OUR DEMOCRATIC TRADITIONS, VALUES, AND LAWS.

WE MUST STOP THEM . . . BEFORE IT'S TOO LATE.

But what do the black helicopters refer to?

The term the "black helicopter crowd" has become a derisive liberal buzz phrase used to categorize those who question the movement for global governance. Anyone who believes that there are currently serious attempts to transfer American autonomy to the United Nations or to an international commission is a labeled as a kook, a conspiracy theorist, a member of the "black helicopter crowd."

Of course, we don't believe that there are actual black helicopters on the way to conquer the United States. But we do believe that the term "black helicopters" is a useful metaphor to capture this attempt to erode our sovereignty by a network of United Nations treaties, codes, guidelines, and other resolutions. We think they have reached a critical mass and that it is time to stop them.

That's what we mean by "Here Come the Black Helicopters!"

CONTENTS

PART ONE

THE FUTURE OF OUR COUNTRY— AND OF OUR FREEDOM—IS IN GRAVE DANGER!

There is a genuine and growing threat to our freedom and autonomy as a nation.

Here's why: The folks at the United Nations and their globalist allies in the United States are determined to take away our national sovereignty. They don't want us to be an independent United States of America—they want us to be just one of the many members of a United States of the World. And they want us to think of ourselves as citizens of the world, not just of the United States.

Make no mistake about it: They are deadly serious about this misguided proposition and they're working night and day to make sure it happens.

Why? Because they think that our existing democratic system is outdated and obsolete in this modern globalized world. They want to replace it with what they believe is a more relevant and all-encompassing worldwide system for governing under the auspices of the United Nations. One that dilutes and negates the power of the United States of America. One that makes each country an equal, regardless of their productivity, population, or economic strength. Under their proposals Monaco, St. Kitts, and the United States would have equal voting power. The Lilliputians will rule the giants.

That's their goal.

They call it "global governance."

We call it the end of freedom. The day when the virtual black helicopters land.

And, believe us, in this case, they are out to create an alternate source of governance—one that we cannot control and one that is meant to homogenize the United States.

So, watch out, the black helicopters are metaphorically on the way.

Where did the name come from?

Well, decades ago, groups opposed to intrusive government actions and those who feared an attempt to create a new world order—with a global government—complained of surveillance by black helicopters, particularly in the western United States. Many of them feared that UN personnel were piloting the helicopters.

In the 1990s, Congresswoman Helen Chenoweth (R-ID) held hearings about the alleged use of black helicopters by the federal Fish & Wildlife Bureau to harass farmers and ranchers in her state. Apparently she was on to something. The Environmental Protection Agency recently admitted that it sanctions unannounced aerial surveillance "flyovers" in order to monitor compliance with the Clean Water Act in the West.[1]

So now the phrase "black helicopter crowd" is used to paint as crackpots anyone who fears government intrusion and usurpation of our national government to a global entity.

The phrase is a favorite propaganda tool of some prominent liberals who use it whenever they want to mock conservatives.

In testimony before the Senate Foreign Relations Committee on May 24, 2012, Secretary of State Hillary Clinton taunted opponents of the controversial Law of the Sea Treaty (one of the top agenda items for the globalists): "[Clinton] chided critics who object to the US joining any UN treaty saying, 'Of course, that means the black helicopters are on their way,' a reference to conspiracy theories about a world government."[2]

Ironically, Clinton's sarcastic remarks were strikingly close to the truth about what is actually happening in the world—with one big exception. There's no secret conspiracy to emasculate the US government and replace its power to govern and regulate with the United Nations and/or independent international commissions.

No, the intention to implement this brazen anti-American coup d'état is way out in the open—right in front of our noses. All we need to do is connect the dots.

And that's what this book will do. We'll discuss in detail exactly what moves are under way to lead us to global governance.

And it's not just Hillary who pejoratively refers to the opponents of "one world government." The *New York Times* recently used the term "black helicopter crowd" in a headline. On July 11, 2012, Eric Pfanner of the *New York Times* wrote an article titled "The Black Helicopter crowd among American geeks has it wrong!" He began his article with "This just in from Geneva: The United Nations has no plans to seize control of the internet. The Web-snatching black helicopters have not left the hangar."[3]

But it turns out that it wasn't the black helicopter crowd who got it wrong—it was the *New York Times* reporter, as we'll document below.

This book will expose the well-formulated scheme to achieve global governance, the plans to emasculate the United States.

The leftists, globalists, and radical environmentalists who advocate this new political alignment deny that they are trying to establish an international government. According to them, their utopian system for planetary decision making is most definitely *not* a plan for a "one-world government"—it's just a plan for global "governance by many agencies and commissions on many issues." Is there really any difference? They also claim that global governance is definitely *not* meant to supersede nation-states or infringe on national sovereignty.

Don't believe them. Not for a minute. Just take a look at what they actually endorse. In 1995, the United Nations' Commission on Global Governance published its final report, titled *Our Global Neighborhood*.[4] This frightening document recommends, among other things:

- Establishing an Economic Security Council to oversee worldwide economies

- Authorizing the United Nations and its agencies to impose global taxes

- Instituting a UN army

- Terminating the veto power of the permanent members of the UN (which, of course, includes the US)

- Creating an International Criminal Court

- Creating a new body of the UN for "civil society," where advocates for the environment, population control, etc., can play a role in policy making

- Placing the authority for regulating the production and distribution of arms in the UN (gun control by another name)

- Granting mandatory jurisdiction in the International Court of Justice for all members. (The US had not accepted this.)

- Ceding jurisdiction over the global commons, such as oceans, space, and the environment, to the Trusteeship Council

Do those sound like the activities of a body that is *not* trying to institute a global government? The power to tax (in this case without representation) as well as to legislate, regulate, and enforce looks strikingly like the powers usually granted to a government. In the United States, we convey those powers to our national government with the understanding that they will be exercised within the framework of our Constitution by public officials elected by and accountable to our citizens.

Global governance will simply create a government body (or bodies), with no democratic underpinnings, run by bureaucrats with no accountability to anyone. That's what they want.

Geographic countries will no longer be important. They see the notion of governing based on sovereign territory or land as old-fashioned, even quaint. As the commission said:

Acknowledging responsibility to something higher than country does not come easily. The impulse to possess turf is a powerful one for all species; yet it is one that people must overcome. In the global neighborhood, a sense of otherness cannot be allowed to nourish instincts of insularity, intolerance, greed, bigotry, and, above all, a desire for dominance. But barricades in the mind can be even more negative than frontiers on the ground. Globalization has made those frontiers increasingly irrelevant.[5]

Apparently, we need to learn just how irrelevant our national boundaries and national government really are, because they seem to envision that we will have to be taught to "acknowledge responsibility" to something beyond our existing government and political institutions.

And as for infringing on national sovereignty, Maurice Strong, an avid socialist except when capitalism benefits him personally,[6] was one of the members of the Commission on Global Governance. Here's what he had this to say about that:

> Sovereignty has been the cornerstone of the interstate system. In an increasingly interdependent world, however, the notions of territoriality, independence, and non-intervention have lost some of their meaning. In certain areas, sovereignty must be exercised collectively, particularly in relation to the global commons.
>
> The principles of sovereignty and non-intervention must be adapted in ways that recognize the need to balance the rights of states with the rights of people, and the interests of nations with the interests of the global neighborhood. It is time also to think about self-determination in the emerging context of a world of separate states.[7]

Does that sound like a statement in support of maintaining independent national governments? Hardly. Not if you know how to read. Consider this: "In certain areas sovereignty needs to be exercised collectively." That seems to be the ultimate oxymoron. Collective sovereignty? It can't exist. (Except in United Nations–speak.) A sovereign nation exerts its own power. It is the opposite of a collective government.

And that is why they want to stop the United States from functioning as a free nation.

We need to keep these folks out of our business and out of our national neighborhood. We must stop them. Because we have no intention of subjecting ourselves to their socialist nanny state. They are still pushing for the very same proposals they made in 1995—and even more.

This is not a proposal by a bunch of fringe liberals. This is a well-organized international movement, to change the world, to minimize the importance of our country, and to regulate our personal behavior, which has been growing over the past twenty years.

And, unfortunately, the Obama administration is among its allies.

The Europeans have long supported the concept of giving up sovereignty. That's what the European Union is all about. And they've also been supportive of global governance. On November 20, 2000, in a speech at The Hague, then French president Jacques Chirac gave a seminal speech celebrating the United Nations' Kyoto Protocol as the first step toward global governance.

> For the first time, humanity is instituting a genuine instrument of global governance. . . . From the very earliest age, we should make environmental awareness a major theme of education and a major theme of political debate, until respect for the environment comes to be as fundamental as safeguarding our rights and freedoms. By acting together, by building this unprecedented instrument, the first component of authentic global governance, we are working for dialogue and peace.[8]

In a speech at Oxford, England, in 2009, former vice president and Nobel Prize winner Al Gore told his audience that he brought good news from America—that the passage of cap-and-trade legislation and the awareness of it "will drive the change, and one of the ways it will drive the change is through global government and global agreements."[9]

There are other buzzwords for global governance. Bill Clinton calls it "interdependence." Through his William J. Clinton Foundation, he supports global governance under the rubric of interdependence and spends more than $100 million each year to promote this euphemism for global governance.

Some well-known liberal supporters believe that the fight is over, that some form of global governance is inevitable.

Strobe Talbott, former Clinton administration undersecretary of state and head of the Brookings Institution, insists that "individual states will increasingly see it in their interest to form an international system that is far more cohesive, far more empowered by its members, and therefore far more effective than the one we have today." [10]

America to Strobe: Some of us actually believe that our current system of democratic government with its guaranteed freedoms and liberty is far more effective than anything you and the United Nations can dream up. Maybe it's time for you to go back to your ivory tower and read our Declaration of Independence and the Constitution.

And noted economist Professor Jeffrey Sachs, head of the Earth Institute at Columbia University and a staunch believer in the need for cooperative global action, has predicted that "[t]he very idea of competing nation-states that scramble for markets, power and resources will become passé." [11]

Passé? Competing nation-states will become passé? Some people seriously doubt that, Professor.

So what exactly is global governance?

Global governance is nothing less than a massive and audacious power grab by the United Nations, an attempt to redefine the world order. But, unfortunately, it's not just our power that they're after—they want to take our wealth, our assets, and our technology, too! And they intend to take them and redistribute them to the poorer, less successful countries of the world.

They think that we owe it to them.

And that's not all. They want to control our land-use planning and our consumption of food and energy. That's because we're the cause of all of the planet's environmental problems.

They have big plans for how they are going to change our ways. Here's what Maurice Strong, the socialist architect and primary advocate of this new global governance doctrine, and who is considered to be the "godfather"[12] of the modern environmental movement, told the opening session of the Rio "Earth Summit" in 1992 about his view of what we have to change:

> [Industrialized countries have] developed and benefited from the unsustainable patterns of production and consumption which have produced our present dilemma. It is clear that current lifestyles and consumption patterns of the affluent middle class involving high meat intake, consumption of large amounts of frozen and convenience foods, use of fossil fuels, appliances, home and work—place air conditioning, and suburban housing—are not sustainable. A shift is necessary toward lifestyles less geared to environmentally damaging consumption patterns.[13]

For the past forty years, Strong, a former undersecretary-general of the UN, has been at the epicenter of just about every conference, commission, meeting, and agenda that has proposed and advocated population control, global governance, and radical environmentalism. He was a member of the Club of Rome, he represented Canada on the Commission for Global Growth, and he was the secretary-general of both the Stockholm and Rio environmental conferences, and was the first director of the United Nations Environmental Programme. Strong was the leading force behind the Kyoto Protocol, and, along with Mikhail Gorbochev, he co-authored *The Earth Charter*, a controversial document that was criticized as the blueprint for one-world socialism. (The charter expanded the rights of man and included the rights of others on the planet, such as rivers and mountains.) His distinguished career at the UN ended in a most undistinguished way in 1997. According to the *Wall Street Journal*:

Evidence procured by federal investigators and the U.N.-authorized inquiry of Paul Volcker showed that Mr. Strong in 1997, while working for Mr. Annan, had endorsed a check for $988,885, made out to "Mr. M. Strong," issued by a Jordanian bank. This check was hand-delivered to Mr. Strong by a South Korean businessman, Tongsun Park, who in 2006 was convicted in New York federal court of conspiring to bribe U.N. officials to rig Oil-for-Food in favor of Saddam.

Mr. Strong was never accused of any wrongdoing. Asked by investigators about the check, he initially denied he'd ever handled it. When they showed it to him with his own signature on the back, he acknowledged that he must have endorsed it, but said the money was meant to cover an investment Mr. Park wished to make in a Strong family company, Cordex, run by one of his sons. (Cordex soon afterward went bankrupt.) Mr. Volcker, in his final report, said that the U.N. might want to "address the need for a more rigorous disclosure process for conflicts of interest." [14]

Strong left the UN and spends most of his time in China, where he advises the Chinese government, teaches at Chinese universities, and advises Chinese businesses. In 1995, at the time the allegations against Strong were made, he was a United Nations Special Envoy to South Korea. According to the *New York Times*, Strong "stepped aside from his post . . . because of past associations with Mr. Park." His contract wasn't renewed.[15]

He lives in Beijing. Strong is a favorite of the Chinese. He was instrumental in drafting and negotiating the Kyoto Protocol, which excluded China (and India) from the carbon-reduction requirements. Recently, the Chinese paid for him to attend the Rio+20 Conference.

Maurice Strong is one of the pilots on the imaginary black helicopters. If he had his way, they'd be landing at this moment.

And, by the way, in the above quote Strong was talking about us— Americans—and he obviously doesn't approve of how we live. So

Strong and his cohorts want us to move out of rural areas, clear out of the suburbs, stop driving cars, and stop using appliances! They want to control how we live, what we eat, how we use our property.

In short, they want to emasculate our ability to self-govern and, instead, impose an international rule of law that is designed to operate against our national interests, violate our democratic ideals and history, and make us subservient to the radical socialist policies of the United Nations and its agencies.

An international law that will find no subject, no issue, no practice too unimportant to focus on. These are not just big-picture folks; they are small-picture folks, too. They want to regulate and control our every action. So, in addition to their major political agenda, they also want to zero in on personal behavior. Think of New York City mayor Michael Bloomberg's ban on the use of salt in restaurants and his proposal to prohibit the sale of large-size sodas. That's the kind of thing they want to regulate on a global basis.

And, unfortunately, these lofty goals for a one-world governance are not just idealistic daydreams. To the contrary, they are part of a carefully designed blueprint for changing the world order and changing the way we think, live, work, and make policy decisions.

Because they can't tolerate the United States as a free and democratic country. We won't conform to their crazy agenda.

They can't tolerate individual freedom. It's too unruly.

That's why their goal is to obliterate the United States of America as we know it—to turn our democracy on its head, and impose a government—or governance—that regulates our every private and personal action.

There's no question about it: They don't want the United States to be an independent, influential, successful—and, yes, powerful—nation that makes its own decisions. Instead, they want us to be part of a "global governance" where we are just one of the many other countries in the world—and just one of the many votes. A global governance that is anti-American.

Here's more from Maurice Strong, about the long-term fate of national sovereignty:

> The concept of national sovereignty has been an immutable, indeed sacred, principle of international relations. It is a principle which will yield only slowly and reluctantly to the new imperatives of global environmental cooperation. What is needed is recognition of the reality that in so many fields, and this is particularly true of environmental issues, it is simply not feasible for sovereignty to be exercised unilaterally by individual nation-states, however powerful. The global community must be assured of environmental security.[16]

Not feasible? It is "not feasible" for countries to exercise their sovereign power to regulate their own country—when it comes to the environment or the many other "fields" that Strong and his comrades identify?

Really?

What is not feasible about the ability of the United States of America to legislate, regulate, and enforce its own environmental laws? (We're taking some liberties here—and assuming that the "however powerful" was a direct reference to the United States.)

Of course, it's feasible.

The only thing that's not feasible about it is that the United States would adapt the radical confiscatory and punitive policies that Strong and his sidekicks recommend.

The only thing that's not feasible is that we would ignore our constitutional protections for private property and individual liberty.

That's what's not feasible.

And that's why the globalists at the United Nations want to take the power to govern our own country on environmental and other issues.

Because it's not feasible that we will adopt the crazy policies that they want.

And it's also not feasible that we will change our system of government to accommodate them.

That's why our existence is such a threat—because we refuse to conform to their view of the world and they cannot stand that.

Global governance is a menace to our nation's liberty, democracy, and sovereignty. Although the ongoing attempts to formalize global governance have heightened recently, the mainstream media has paid little or no attention to what is unfolding. Because of that, this scary scheme is advancing in stealth. Perhaps the media have not connected the dots. This massive power grab by the United Nations is scarcely attracting any comment, much less any opposition. Yet the threat is imminent and immediate.

This book will connect the dots. It will spell out the carefully choreographed plan to empower the unelected, undemocratic, unaccountable United Nations as the director of the new global governance.

The blueprint for this was drawn many years ago and it is only recently that the socialists' dream has come close to fruition.

For all of us, it is urgent that we act now.

Before it's too late.

Because, right now, right in front of us, there is a frightening worldwide movement—spearheaded by liberals, socialists, globalists, and radical environmentalists. They want to dominate us globally by seriously limiting our freedom, forcibly changing our lifestyles, emasculating our democratic institutions, redistributing our wealth, assets, and technology to poorer countries, and subjecting us to an international rule of law imposed by the United Nations.

A rule of law that will be directed by faceless and unaccountable bureaucrats.

A rule of law that is antithetical to our representative system of government.

A rule of law that is based on a socialist philosophy.

A rule of law that stems from an anti-American bias.

A rule of law that we cannot tolerate.

In short, these globalists and socialists want to reorganize the world into an easily managed and cohesive group of nations who willingly cede their sovereignty to a series of international organizations associated with the United Nations. That is exactly what they intend to do.

And it's just around the corner. So is the end of freedom if they succeed.

Global governance, at its core, is a process of decision making that is intended to systematically undermine the sovereignty and authority of productive and successful nations like the United States and Japan. That's what it's all about.

The central organizing tool for the imposition of one-world global governance has been the worldwide environmental movement to overcome the assumed dangers of climate change.

Whether you subscribe to the existence of global warming and the need to protect the planet is not relevant to this threat. Nor is the issue of whether climate change is man-made. Those are not the issues today. What is the issue is that, since its inception, many of the most important leaders of the planetary global warming movement have capitalized on widespread fear of the consequences of global warming (fears that, for the most part, were created by them) to systematically and aggressively advance their goal of global governance and scare people into believing their new international system is the only hope for the future of the planet.

Advancing in the name of environmentalism, social justice, and sustainability, the globalists and socialists—who run the United Nations—are proceeding apace with their far-reaching game plan to end national sovereignty and subsume all nations under global governance. Focusing on what they have identified as "planetary" environmental problems, such as climate change and ocean acidification, they are determined to implement an agenda of socialist central planning to curb the power of democratic electorates and the sovereignty of nation-states, and force them into a global regulatory scheme.

Their stated goals are to reverse climate change, reduce carbon emissions, increase living standards in the impoverished Southern Hemisphere, and make development sustainable in an era of limited and diminishing natural resources.

But it's a mask.

However much the globalists believe in environmental reforms, their real goal is to establish a one-world government—dominated by self-selected elites—that will preempt nations and their electorates and force them to abide by regulations promulgated by rulers over whom they have no say or control. Just as Karl Marx called for a global government of the working class, so they want one of economists, social scientists, environmentalists, and other self-chosen quasi-academic elites. Just as Marx used the poverty of the labor force in nineteenth-century capitalism as his touchstone in formulating his plans, so they use the supposed threats to the global environment as theirs.

Broadly, there are two political philosophy camps in the world: those who believe in free markets and individual liberty and those who believe in central planning and dictation from above. The believers in freedom root their conviction that free people, free markets, and free competition will steer the world in the right direction, with public education substituting for central planning and direction. To the freedom advocates, it is through economic and political freedom that progress is possible. To the top-down globalists and planners, it is an impediment that gets in the way of wiser heads directing the planet.

The apostle of economic and political liberty, Friedrich Hayek, described in his famous work, *The Road to Serfdom*, at the end of World War II a dichotomy in which he lumped communism, socialism, fascism, and Nazism together as the opponents of liberal democratic freedom. His contrast between planning and competition, centralization and freedom, were valid then and are even more so today.

As Hayek put it, "We have seen before how the separation of economic and political aims is an essential guarantee of individual freedom and how it is consequently attacked by all collectivists. To this we must now add the 'substitution of political for economic power' now so often demanded means necessarily the substitution of power from which there is no escape for power which is always limited." [17]

Hayek was prescient in foreseeing the result of collectivism, planning, and total political power: "What is called economic power, while it can be an instrument of coercion, is, in the hands of private individuals, never exclusive or complete power, never power over the whole life of a person. But centralized as an instrument of political power, it creates a degree of dependence scarcely distinguishable from slavery." [18]

Hayek predicted that the forces of tyranny would advance by wrapping their lust for power in a sacred cause. Citing the requisites of that objective, they would insist that all conform to their plans to advance it, overriding individual choice and market economics.

This is exactly what has happened in the global governance movement. The push for a one-world order has been wrapped around saving the planet from the effects of global warming.

To some, the objective of central planning was national honor and military victory. Others, justified totalitarian rule by saying it aimed for the global victory of the working class (but it became increasingly evident that the objectives were traditional imperialism and the expansion of national power).

The modern-day globalists and greens use the cause of reversing climate change and "saving" our planetary environment as their justification for global planning and control.

But their objective, too, is quite clear: global control and power. And just like their forebears, their real enemy is not climate change or carbon emissions but the liberal, free market democracies and the rule of sovereign electorates. Like them, they must organize all in the name of their cause to make democratic rule irrelevant and obsolete.

Hayek specifically warns about such prophets:

The movement for planning owes its present strength largely to the fact that . . . it unites almost all the single minded idealists, all the men and women who have devoted their lives to a single task. The hopes they place in planning, however, are the result . . . of great exaggeration of the importance of the ends they place foremost. . . . From the saintly and single minded idealist to the fanatic is often but a single step. It is the resentment of the frustrated specialist which gives the demand for planning its strongest impetus. There could hardly be a more unbearable and more irrational world than one in which the most eminent specialists in each field were allowed to proceed unchecked with the realization of their ideals.[19]

Hayek's description fits today's radical environmentalists to a T. Obsessed by their conviction that the planet is coming to an end, they insist that all nations, states, localities, communities, families, and people submit to a discipline they would impose on every aspect of their lives in order to save us from destruction. But what they end up doing is canceling out both free will for the individual and democratic determination of policies for the nation. Only their fetish has priority. Nothing else matters. All must fall in line behind their plan for the world.

Our modern-day globalists/socialists/radical environmentalists have laid out a program of worldwide change to achieve "sustainability." By that they mean an end to the man-made causes of global climate change on the one hand and a transfer of wealth from developed to developing nations on the other. By linking the two causes, they try to enlist the support of the green enthusiasts in rich countries and the backing of the autocracies and dictatorships that dominate the third world.

The organizing path that followed was revealed in 1991 in *The First Global Revolution*, published by the Club of Rome. Among the Club's notable members are many of the world's foremost leaders, including David Rockefeller, former president Jimmy Carter, former vice president Al Gore, former Soviet leader Mikhail Gorbachev, the king of Spain Juan Carlos, former Canadian prime minister Pierre Trudeau, former Brazilian president Fernando Enrique Cardozo, former Mexican president Ernesto Zedillo, and Maurice Strong.[20]

The Club, founded in 1968, describes itself as "an informal association of independent leading personalities from politics, business and science . . . [who] share a common concern for the future of humanity and the planet." [21] That's an understatement.

In 1972, the Club published *The Limits of Growth*, a provocative book that painted a drastic picture of the inability of the planet to sustain itself unless the world population was seriously curtailed and natural resources preserved. Based on computer models of the future, the book caught the attention of the world, selling more than 12 million copies, and marked the beginning of the international focus on the need to protect the environment.

It also scared people to death with its message of gloom and doom and the end of the planet. In retrospect, that was the plan—to frighten people about the need for population control and the shepherding of resources so that global governance could emerge.

In *The First Global Revolution*, the authors presented a clear, unabashed outline of the globalist/socialist/radical environmentalist game plan to end free markets and replace democracy by hyping—and inventing—environmental concerns. It was in this book that the authors articulated the strategic need to create a common enemy to unite diverse peoples behind a worldwide cause.

They concluded that we need common enemies to motivate us to make big changes: "a common adversary, to organize and act together . . . such a motivation must be found to bring the divided nations together to face an outside enemy. . . ." [22]

This enemy need not be real, the authors postulate. It can be "either a real one or else one invented for the purpose. . . . This is the way we are setting the scene for mankind's encounter with the planet. New enemies therefore have to be identified. New strategies imagined, new weapons devised." [23]

Then they report—as if a lightbulb went off in their minds—that they have reached a consensus on what the new enemy is to be: "In searching for a new enemy to unite us, we came up with the idea that pollution, the threat of global warming, water shortages, famine and the like would fit the bill. All these dangers are caused by human intervention, and it is only through changed attitudes and behavior that they can be overcome. The real enemy then, is humanity itself." [24]

This was the beginning of the use of the movement for climate change to achieve global governance.

It's worth noting that the character of the Club of Rome, its members, and its work on global governance practically invites speculation about conspiracy theories. It presents all the elements of a Robert Ludlum book or a James Bond movie. All that's missing is the white cat from the James Bond movies. Consider this: The Club was founded at a villa outside Rome, purportedly owned by David Rockefeller, one of its original members. His father, John D. Rockefeller Jr., donated the land where the United Nations sits in New York City. David, the billionaire banker, philanthropist, member of the Council on Foreign Relations, and founder of the Trilateral Commission, was a longtime advocate of global governance, as he discloses in his memoirs:

> For more than a century ideological extremists at either end of the political spectrum have seized upon well-publicized incidents such as my encounter with Castro to attack the Rockefeller family for the inordinate influence they claim we wield over American political and economic institutions. Some even believe we are part of a secret cabal working against the best interests of the United States, characterizing my family and me as internationalists and of conspiring with others around the world to build a more integrated global political and economic structure—one world, if you will. If that's the charge, I stand guilty, and I am proud of it. [25]

Rockefeller's friendship with Henry Kissinger, Gorbachev, Maurice Strong, and other globalists, as well as his well-documented support for a one-world order, led to rampant conspiracy theories about the group and its work.

Because the Club of Rome was certainly proposing global governance. Alas, according to *The First Global Revolution*, the requisites of the moment will force us to discard the old-fashioned notion of democracy and consent of the governed: "The old democracies have functioned reasonably well over the last 200 years, but they appear now to be in a phase of complacent stagnation with little evidence of real leadership and innovation."

Our new would-be rulers note that "democracy is not a panacea. It cannot organize everything and it is unaware of its own limits. These facts must be faced squarely."

These people are serious. They do not want a United States of America and its democratic form of government. To them, a government of the people, by the people, and for the people fails their test: "Sacrilegious though this may sound, democracy is no longer well suited for the tasks ahead. The complexity and the technical nature of many of today's problems do not always allow elected representatives to make competent decisions at the right time."[26]

Fundamental to this worldview is the elevation of the bureaucrat, the planner, and the expert over the free market entrepreneur in search of profit. The expert who never sees, never speaks to, and doesn't care about the electorate. Hayek notes that this hierarchy has characterized European thinking for centuries. He writes of the

> deliberate disparagement of all activities involving economic risk and the moral opprobrium cast on the gains which make risks worth taking but which only few can win. We cannot blame our young men when they prefer the safe, salaried position to the risk of enterprise after they have heard from their earliest youth the former described as the superior, more unselfish and disinterested occupation. The younger generation of today has grown up in a world in which in school and press the spirit of commercial enterprise has been represented as disreputable and the making of profit as immoral, where to employ a hundred people is represented as exploitation but to command the same number is honorable.[27]

Elsewhere in *The Global Revolution*, the Club makes explicit its manipulation of environmentalism to achieve its purposes: "In searching for a new enemy to unite us, we came up with the idea that pollution, the threat of global warming, water shortages, famine, and the like would fill the bill. All these dangers are caused by human intervention and it is only through changed attitudes and behavior that they can be overcome."

The advocates of global governance want to get rid of democratic governments with national elections. Once again, here's Mr. Strong with his view of what we need: "Our concepts of ballot-box democracy may need to be modified to produce strong governments capable of making difficult decisions."[28]

Apparently decisions that are made by representative governments are not really decisions. Only decisions made by a global consensus without any accountability are valid.

That's what we are up against.

Because it is rooted in the radical environmental movement, and because of its socialist origins, one of the key goals of the planned global governance is the worldwide redistribution of wealth, assets, and technology from rich countries to poor countries. Part of that is about reparation, the demand that we pay for our dual sins of pollution and consumption. Part of it is simply a manifestation of the socialist ideology that social ownership of the assets and resources of the planet is a necessity for a global economy. So, although we produce 25 percent of the world's wealth, they want to decide just how much of that they'll let us keep.

The movement to consolidate national sovereignty into global governance began—in the modern era—in the late 1960s with the founding of the Club of Rome, but it has been a constant and growing obsession of the left ever since.

Inherent in it is a desire to get the power to tax our wealth. However they rationalize their scheme, it still comes down to this: They want our money. They want our assets. They want the ability to tax us. They want us to give them our technology, developed by our creative entre-preneurs, often with government investments.

On Thursday, July 5, 2012—the day after our celebration of national independence—the UN called for a global tax on billionaires, intended to raise more than $400 billion a year for the world's poor countries. The proposal would tax 1,226 billionaires to raise the money (425 of whom live in the US). The tax proposal is coupled with four other pro-posed global taxes—each imposed by the UN:

- [A] tax of $25 per tonne on carbon dioxide emissions would raise about $250 billion. It could be collected by national governments, but allocated to international cooperation.

- [A] tax of 0.005 percent on all currency transactions in the dollar, yen, euro and pound sterling could raise $40 billion a year.

- [T]aking a portion of a proposed European Union tax on financial transactions for international cooperation. The tax is expected to raise more than $70 billion a year.[29]

It also suggests expanding a levy on air tickets that a number of na-tions already impose to raise money for drugs for poor states through UNITAID, a UN initiative.

In its extreme, global governance also wants to eventually eliminate national elections, especially in the United States. They see the con-cept of popular elections as an unnecessary evil, which often leads to elected officials actually responding to the demands of their constitu-ents. Imagine that! Some would call that the hallmark of democracy. This quote from Columbia economist Jeffrey Sachs indicates just how naive and nutty these folks can be: "The prevailing unilateralism of the United States will seem for many people to be an inevitable feature of world politics in which politicians are voted in or out of office by their own populations rather than by a global electorate." [30]

While this is undoubtedly the view of the global governance crowd, most of them are afraid to say just how far they want to go to destroy our political system.

It's hard to understand exactly what Professor Sachs is really saying. Is he proposing that politicians in the United States should be elected by a global electorate? That seems too far-fetched for even the global governance zealots. More likely he is suggesting that we elect a worldwide government that is not answerable to us.

Think about it: A global governance would eliminate the troublesome dictates of the US Constitution, as well as unruly citizen participation and dialogue. It would stymie the ability of duly elected American officials to determine our policies, and would tax us without representation.

The plan essentially calls for a dumbing down of America and a leveling of American influence and ideology.

How will these goals be realized?

By enforcing obscure treaties that bind us to outrageous mandates without the participation of Congress and without the consent of our people. (We'll discuss this in detail below.)

By international conferences with implementing agendas—like the Rio environmental conferences—and signed agreements that often include criminal sanctions.

By imposing international taxes without our consent.

The idealized concept of one-world government has been kicking around for a long time. Its genesis is deeply imbedded in socialist principles. Currently disguised in contemporary United Nations globalspeak, it relies on "sustainability" as the unifying theme.

Sustainability purportedly means that planetary growth and development must only advance if it does not impair the sustainability of the planet. But *sustainability* is really just a buzzword for a massive redistribution of wealth from democracies like the United States—where hardworking people are productive and build assets—to third world countries whose leaders are often corrupt dictators who ignore the dire conditions of their fellow countrymen, who often neither work nor produce.

Recently, there has been a frenetic push by the "international community" to make this unwise and undemocratic policy come true.

Even the Vatican has weighed in, recently calling for a one-world government: "Globalization, despite some of its negative aspects, is unifying peoples more and prompting them to move towards a new 'rule of law' on the supranational level, supported by a more intense and fruitful collaboration."[31]

This view of the need for a "supranational" level of government is, unfortunately, shared by many. These are the people and organizations who want us to surrender our national identity, change our lifestyles, provide reparations for what they view as our excesses, and surrender to a new order of international institutions that will tell us what to do, when to do it, and how much to pay for it.

How will they be able to transfer our wealth? By imposing mandatory foreign aid to underdeveloped countries and by enacting international taxes aimed at the United States, including carbon taxes, airline taxes, and Internet taxes. And we'll have no way to stop them.

And that's not all. They also want to require us to hand over our technology—our valuable intellectual property—to countries who don't have either the brain power or the financial resources to develop their own.

All of this is called social justice. More like economic injustice.

They want to take major decision making away from the Congress and Executive Branch and replace it, instead, with a one-world governing system.

And the Obama administration is helping them do it by rushing through a series of treaties that will transfer sovereign power and control to global agencies.

Barack Obama believes in it. Think about it: We have a president who goes to the United Nations to ask for permission to bring a military action in Libya, but claims that he isn't required to seek the approval of the United States Congress under the War Powers Act—even when his own Department of Justice advises him that he is required to do so.

There's no doubt about it: President Obama embraces the one-world global view. So does his secretary of state, Hillary Clinton.

Obama showed his hand even before he was president. On July 24, 2008, then–US senator Barack Obama spoke to the largest crowd of the presidential campaign in Berlin, Germany. More than two hundred thousand people thronged into the park in front of the site where the Berlin Wall, separating East and West Germany, communism and freedom, had once stood. All were anxious to hear the young senator who was stirring the American electorate and who might be an antidote to President George W. Bush, who was detested by Europeans.

The spectators got what they came for. Obama talked the talk, walked the walk. He spoke their language. Playing to the crowd, he told them that he came to Berlin not as a presidential candidate, but as a "citizen of the world." His rhetoric soared as he repeatedly spoke of "global cooperation," "global partnership," "global commitment," and the "burden of global citizenship" . . . that continue[s] to bind us together." [32]

"I speak as a citizen of the world," he told the crowd. [33]

Those few words, emphasizing Obama's obvious embrace of globalism and global governance over nationalism, foretold his vision of a new world order. In this new paradigm, America is just one part of a worldwide decision-making process, instead of an independent—and, yes, nationalistic—country with historic political and cultural roots set deep in democracy that are often at odds with some of the rest of the world, including Europe.

This book is a wake-up call to all Americans who value our democratic traditions and culture, who still believe in the fundamental tenets of liberty and freedom that are the cornerstones of our great nation, and who applaud the uniqueness of America.

WHY GLOBAL GOVERNMENT WILL NOT
BE ACCEPTED BY AMERICANS

David Brooks of the *New York Times* cited five reasons why Americans will never accept what he calls the "vaporous global-governance notion." [34]

We'll never accept it, first, because it is undemocratic. It is impossible to set up legitimate global authorities because there is no global democracy, no sense of common peoplehood and trust. So multilateral organizations can never look like legislatures, with open debate, up or down votes, and the losers accepting majority decisions.

Instead, they look like meetings of unelected elites, of technocrats who make decisions in secret and who rely upon intentionally impenetrable language, who settle differences through arcane fudges. Americans, like most peoples, will never surrender even a bit of their national democracy for the sake of multilateral technocracy.

Second, we will never accept global governance because it inevitably devolves into corruption. The panoply of UN scandals flows from a single source: the lack of democratic accountability. These supranational organizations exist in their own insular, self-indulgent aerie.

We will never accept global governance, third, because we love our Constitution and will never grant any other law supremacy over it. Like most peoples (Europeans are the exception), we will never allow transnational organizations to overrule our own laws, regulations and precedents. We think our Constitution is superior to the sloppy authority granted to, say, the International Criminal Court.

Fourth, we understand that these mushy international organizations liberate the barbaric and handcuff the civilized. Bodies like the U.N. can toss hapless resolutions at the Milosevices, the Saddams, or the butchers of Darfur, but they can do nothing to restrain them. Meanwhile, the forces of decency can be paralyzed as they wait for "the international community."

Fifth, we know that when push comes to shove, all the grand talk about international norms is often just a cover for opposing the global elite's bêtes noires of the moment—usually the U.S. or Israel. We will never grant legitimacy to forums that are so often manipulated for partisan ends.[35]

David Brooks is right, but there's more. As a nation of states, it took us a long time to become a cohesive nation, trustful of all our fellow citizens. Indeed, before the American people came to trust one another fully in sharing our national sovereignty, we went through a cleansing process from 1861 to 1865—the American Civil War. As Abraham Lincoln famously said, we could no longer exist "half slave and half free." He quoted the biblical prophecy that "a house divided against itself cannot stand."

The states of the North—led by the unerring moral compass of the abolitionists—rejected the idea that they would have to share their country with slaveholders and the vast, feudal, class-conscious estates they ruled. The "slave power" became the enemy of the North and people of conscience were determined to purge it from America.

And they did.

As with the United Nations' General Assembly, the slave power perpetuated its rule through the principle of one-state, one-vote in the US Senate. Southern defenders of slavery made sure that the number of free and slave states were equal so that they would not be outvoted in the Senate (increased population growth in the North made the House of Representatives an increasingly antislavery institution). Whenever a free state was admitted to the Union, for example Maine in 1820, a slave state (in 1820, Missouri) would be let in to offset it. When the Supreme Court ruled—in the Dred Scott decision of 1857—that Congress could not bar slavery in any territory, it led directly to the Civil War. The North would not subsist in a nation that permanently tolerated the spread of slavery.

Even in modern times, the civil rights movement fought to extirpate racial segregation from the southern states, eventually bringing them into conformity with the racial integration (sort of) practiced in the North.

Don't we have a similar duty? Mustn't we make sure that we are entering a world of free nations based on the rule of law, integrity, and respect for human rights that we fought so hard for before we sign away our sovereignty? That is not to say that we should undertake any global crusade to liberate and improve the world. But it is to say that we should look before we leap and check out to what kind of countries we are ceding our sovereignty.

Do we want to be in a global ruling partnership with Russia, China, or a collection of tiny, lightly populated, third world autocracies, riddled with corruption and dedicated to the enrichment of their leaders? These are not the kind of bedfellows we want in our government. They are not worthy of entrusting our sovereignty to them.

And we will not accept them.

Join us in this urgent fight to maintain our sovereignty and stop the forces of global governance.

But, if you do, be prepared to be identified as one of the "black helicopter crowd."

You'll be in good company.

TREATIES: HOW THE OBAMA ADMINISTRATION WANTS TO UNDERMINE OUR SOVEREIGNTY

UN treaties are a favorite way of circumventing our national government and transferring our power, control, and resources to a new global entity. And the Obama administration is determined to destroy the very essence of our national sovereignty and transfer power from our elected Congress to the UN General Assembly—a body filled with corrupt, undemocratic, tyrannical nations that abuse human rights and do not share our values.

If Barack Obama is reelected in November 2012, his agenda for global governance through the United Nations will pick up steam. But even if he is defeated—or especially if he is defeated—he and his outgoing secretary of state, Hillary Clinton, are planning to use his remaining months in office to sign a series of treaties and international protocols that will bind our country for decades to come. We need to remember one fundamental but little known fact: Any treaty signed by the US but not yet ratified by the Senate is binding on our country—as if it had been ratified—until it is either rejected by the Senate or renounced by the president. This requirement—embedded in the Vienna Convention signed and ratified by the US—means that these treaties might come into force and effect even if we never ratify them.

Frank Gaffney, who was assistant secretary of defense in the Reagan administration and currently heads the Center for Security Policy, explains the curious fact that we are bound by treaties even if we don't ratify them. "The Vienna Convention governing the status of treaties—to which we are a party—requires states that sign a treaty to refrain from any actions that undermine the treaty pending ratification until such time as a formal renunciation of the treaty is made. In practice, this is done by the State Department. This translates into actual compliance with the treaty including often paying the dues we would be obliged to pay once we are parties [to the treaty after ratification]." [36]

Because of the Vienna Convention, Senate Majority Leader Harry Reid need not bring these treaties up for ratification if he feels he lacks the votes to pass them. Then, if the Democrats keep the Senate and Obama is reelected, these treaties will remain in force throughout his second term—never voted down (or up) by the Senate or renounced by the president. Our only remedy then, will be to defeat Obama and/or capture the Senate.

Nevertheless, Obama and Hillary Clinton are very anxious to get as many of these treaties as possible ratified in the lame duck session of Congress, after November but before the results of the 2012 election come into play. Even though some of these treaties have been kicking around for thirty years, they know that this might be their last chance to put into place key elements of their global governance plan.

One other reason that the treaties have become such a high priority is that Senator John Kerry chairs the Senate Foreign Relations Committee and is trying out for the position of next secretary of state. He is anxious to show how he can deliver the left's agenda.

But Obama need not rely on the Vienna Convention since some of these treaties might get through in the lame-duck session of Congress that will meet after the election results are in. Even if the Republicans take control of the Senate, it won't matter at all because it will be the outgoing, defeated Democratic senators who will vote on these treaties. Immunized by their defeats from public pressure—and possibly embittered by their losses—they will willingly vote to hogtie the United States and approve the massive grant of sovereignty to the United Nations.

Obama and Clinton are feverishly negotiating treaties—with very little public attention—and lining up votes for Senate ratification of numerous treaties.

Once these treaties are passed, they are the law of the United States forever.

That's why we need to stop them.

Laws can be repealed, but treaties cannot. The Supremacy Clause of the US Constitution characterizes all treaties as "the supreme law of the land" akin to constitutional provisions. Treaties supersede acts of Congress or of the various state legislatures and American courts are required to enforce these treaties in most instances. There are only two ways to get out of a treaty: (1) if the other signatories let us (all 190 nations that sign them in most cases) or (2) by passing a constitutional amendment.

The treaties Obama and Hillary are rushing to completion will permanently cede vast swaths of our national sovereignty to the UN.

We wrote briefly about these treaties in "Tricks or Treaties," chapter 2 of our previous book, *Screwed!*. But since that book's publication in early May 2012, these threats to our freedom have multiplied and gained momentum even as brand new threats—as that to Internet freedom—have come into public view. So we write this volume to explain the assault against our values and our nationhood so we can act to preserve our country from these threats while there is still time.

Here's what Obama and Hillary are trying to do:

Law of the Sea Treaty

Signed by the president. Up for Senate ratification before the end of the year, it would:

- Give the UN control of the 71 percent of the earth's surface covered by oceans and seas and all minerals and fish underneath.

- It would likely subject the US to international rules on carbon emissions such as the Kyoto Treaty (never ratified by the Senate) and might be used to force us into a global cap-and-trade system.

- It would curb the ability of the US Navy to perform its historic mission of protecting freedom of the seas and vest the power in a tribunal appointed by the UN secretary-general.

- Give the International Seabed Authority—a group of 193 nations in which we would have but one vote—the power to tax offshore oil and gas wells and pay the revenues, at their discretion, to any third world nation it chooses.

- Oblige our oil and gas companies to share, for free, all of our most modern offshore drilling technology.

UN Control of the Internet

A treaty giving the United Nations control over the Internet is now under negotiation (in secret). Responding to proposals by Russia, China, Brazil, and India, the negotiators hope to present a final treaty for signature by the nations of the world at a conference in Dubai in December 2012. It would:

- Give the UN power to regulate online content.

- Allow nations to inspect private email communications by their citizens.

- Permit nations to charge Internet traffic coming in from abroad a fee akin to that charged for long-distance phone calls. So Google, Facebook, Apple, etc., would have to pay tolls to send their content into these nations.

- Give the UN authority to allocate Internet addresses and require it to turn over to member nations (like China) the IP addresses (a unique set of numbers that indicate the geographic location of each and every computer) of each user.

The negotiations are ongoing. The US negotiators will probably succeed in diluting some of these provisions, but the chances for eventual passage of these destructive changes is such that Vinton Cerf, one of the two founders of the Internet, said that the free Internet is now under more threat than ever before.

Gun Control

At a global meeting in New York on July 27, 2012, the nations of the world—including the US—were scheduled sign an Arms Trade Treaty

(ATT), which will empower an international body to regulate the international arms trade. Its goal is eventually to establish a system of worldwide gun control. While paying lip service to the right of private individuals to own, buy, sell, or transfer arms, the body will have a life of its own and the power to require of the signatory nations measures to effectuate the goal of the treaty. These could include gun confiscation and will almost certainly call for universal registration and licensing.

And the global governing body the treaty establishes can pass whatever rules it wants without having to come back to the Senate or to any national legislative body for approval.

The treaty signing was canceled after fifty-one senators said they would oppose its ratification. But it is likely to be approved and finalized by a two-thirds vote of the General Assembly of the UN. Then it would go into effect if ratified by sixty-five nations (easily done). At that point, the US could either sign it or not. If it signed the treaty, we would be bound, under the Vienna Convention, until it was rejected for Senate ratification or renounced by a future president.

The best bet is that Obama signs the treaty after election day and Harry Reid never submits it for ratification so it remains in force until it is either renounced by a President Romney or rejected by a Republican-controlled Senate.

Global Environmentalism

Under the terms of the recently negotiated Rio+20 Treaty, the United Nations Environment Programme, a UN body, will be granted increased power to act as a worldwide Environmental Protection Agency, promulgating global regulations.

The United States will be obliged to contribute to a fund to help third world nations cope with environmental change. At the Rio Conference in June 2012, Secretary of State Clinton pledged $2 billion for this fund, which is expected to reach $100 billion when fully implemented. The

US would have only one vote out of 193 in deciding to which regimes these funds will be paid.

International Criminal Court

This treaty, signed by Clinton and then renounced by President George W. Bush, may be signed again by President Obama during his second term or before he leaves office following an election defeat.

It supersedes the US Supreme Court and makes our entire judicial system subject to the rulings of an international court. The court would have the power to establish the extent of its own jurisdiction and would have the power to adjudicate disputes between Americans on US soil even after the Supreme Court has ruled. Double jeopardy would not attach to its review of American court rulings. The court would not have trial by jury or any of the constitutional protections Americans now enjoy.

Dangerously, it establishes the new global crime of "aggression," which it defines as going to war without UN Security Council approval. US presidents could be prosecuted criminally after they leave office for violating this new law. In practice, of course, this provision would give Russia and China jurisdiction over the use of the US military.

Missile Defense

Under the guise of a "code of conduct" to limit debris in outer space, the Obama administration is negotiating an agreement to limit what satellites or missiles can be put into orbit around the earth. This code is widely seen as a backdoor attempt to reimpose the constraints on defensive anti-missiles embodied in the Anti-Ballistic Missile Treaty (ABM) and renounced by President George W. Bush.

Each of these treaties creates a new global entity charged with its enforcement. Whether it is a gun control agency or a Seabed Authority or an International Criminal Court, these treaties empower such agencies. Long after the treaties have been signed and ratified and after the various disclaimers have been inserted by our diplomats protecting our rights and sovereignty, these agencies will remain, able to expand their jurisdiction, legislate new provisions, impose additional taxes and penalties, and require obedience by the signatories to the treaties that set them up—all without any input from us and all without any accountability to us.

These enforcement agencies will inevitably acquire a life of their own, expanding their powers and eroding our sovereignty at every turn. This trend will not be an unintended consequence of these treaties—the systematic erosion of America's sovereignty and subjecting her wealth and power to global control is quite specifically the intention of these treaties and the people who wrote them.

Each one strips us of control over our own destiny and places our sovereignty under the political control of the United Nations, and not, it must be noted, the Security Council of the UN on which we have a veto. These powers would largely be vested in newly created global bodies in which all of the world's nations—corrupt or not, democratic or not, free or not, tiny and large—would have an equal say.

And then there is the question of who would obey these treaties. Russia, China, Iran, North Korea, and other outlaw nations have shown no regard for their treaty obligations. They each routinely disregard the provisions of the treaties they have signed and feel in no respect bound by them.

By contrast, law-abiding nations like the United States take their treaty obligations very seriously and are scrupulous in carrying them out to the legalistic letter. Indeed, American courts would be obliged—under the Supremacy Clause—to enforce these treaties, honoring them all even as the other nations who sign them take them lightly.

AMERICA'S TREATY ADDICTION

What is it with our diplomats? Why do they constantly seek to ensnare us in treaties to regulate each aspect of our existence? Can't our diplomats ever say no?

Our foreign policy is largely conducted by globalists who work within our State Department, and the National Security Council. Deeply committed to the one-world agenda, they have dedicated their lives and public service to bringing the UStates into the global fold. The goals of the Club of Rome have no greater allies than many of the men and women of our foreign service.

Our nation's foreign affairs experts live in the shadow of the trauma of the United States' rejection of the Treaty of Versailles ending World War I and establishing the League of Nations. Because of the United States' refusal to enter the global body and the perpetuation of American isolationism, historians assign to the United States much of the blame for the failed peace that followed the First World War and led directly to the second.

These experts fear the resurgence of isolationism and are determined to ensure that the United States is a full participant in every global treaty that comes down the pike.

When President Woodrow Wilson led the United States into the war in 1917—until then a conflict of Britain, France, and Russia against Germany and Austro-Hungary—he promised that it would be "a war to end all wars." When the American military began to weigh heavily into the scales of the conflict, eventually forcing a German surrender in 1918, the president amplified his idealistic motivation for fighting by issuing his "Fourteen Points," which would be the basis for what he described as "a peace without victory."

The document that set forth Wilson's Fourteen Points was one of the most idealistic in diplomatic history. It pledged the nations of the world to postwar boundaries based on self-determination by each country's people. Every ethnic or national group would be able to determine, democratically, to which country they wished to belong. Freedom of the seas, the rights of neutral nations, and free flow of commerce were guaranteed. And, to enforce and implement this program, a League of Nations was to be established.

When the Armistice ending the war was signed—largely based on German acceptance of the Fourteen Points—Wilson sailed to Europe to attend a peace conference at the French palace of Versailles, where the nations of the world gathered. While all the Allied powers, who dictated the peace to Germany and its defeated allies, paid lip service to the Fourteen Points, they disregarded it when it came to thrashing out the details of the peace settlement.

When the final document emerged, nobody was happy. The ideal of self-determination was breached more than it was honored. The treaty reflected the same mad scramble for territory and reparations that had always accompanied the end of wars. This was far from a war to end all wars. In fact, it was the beginning of the onset of World War II!

Of all Wilson's Fourteen Points only the provision for a League of Nations emerged in the final draft of the Treaty of Versailles. But when the document came up for ratification in the Republican-dominated US Senate, it was harshly criticized and ultimately rejected. So Wilson's League began operations without the United States in attendance. The US never joined and played almost no role in trying to keep the peace between the world wars. With isolationists firmly in control of our foreign policy throughout the twenties, the United States turned inward and let the world hurdle toward another ghastly war.

When finally war came, first to Asia in 1934, to Europe in 1939 and to the US in 1941, it was a global catastrophe. More than fifty million lay dead by its end.

Determined to avoid the isolationism that had engulfed the United States at the end of World War I, Presidents Roosevelt and Truman firmly steered the US into the UN and raised great hopes for its effectiveness. Our diplomats, chastened by our former isolationism, determined that they would never again sit on the sidelines. Having "a seat at the table" became a mantra on Capitol Hill and in the State and Defense departments. Never again would we shut ourselves out.

The legacy of this harsh lesson still carries over. American diplomats instinctively rally to the negotiating table wherever it is, whatever it is about. The rest of the world understands that without American participation, no agreement is worth the paper on which it is written. And the other nations use the treaty-making process primarily as a way to cut the United States down to size. But the addiction of our foreign policy establishment to international conventions, forums, negotiations, and debates ensures our presence at the table and, most likely, our ascension to the global consensus.

But now the time has come for us to be left out; more precisely, to opt out of negotiations that can only lead to a loss of our sovereignty and to the undermining of our democratic system of government. From all sides, we face the pressures of a global community terrified by our power, humbled by our success, and determined to rein us in by ensnaring us in treaties and limitations of all sorts and sizes. What they could never hope to accomplish by military force or by economic power, these nations hope to accomplish by negotiation and treaty. Bluntly, they want to inveigle our gullible diplomats into signing away our country's rights. As the old saying goes: Uncle Sam has never lost a war nor won a conference.

Now let's look at each of these treaties in depth. Let's see how they chip, chip, chip away at our national sovereignty and our democratic self-government.

PART TWO

UN FORCES GUN CONTROL ON AMERICA

The Second Amendment to the US Constitution, granting our citizens the right to bear arms, may be facing de facto repeal in the Arms Trade Treaty now being pushed by the UN.

Have you noticed that President Obama has used his term in office to push every item on the liberal agenda except for gun control? During the 2008 campaign, he spoke of embittered Americans who "cling to their guns," [1] but hasn't spoken of the issue much since.

Now it's clear why he hasn't. He plans to accomplish the liberal agenda of registering, banning, and ultimately confiscating guns through an Arms Trade Treaty (ATT).

At this writing, the treaty's precise terms have not been unveiled, but its intent is crystal clear: to repeal our Second Amendment and limit or eliminate the right to bear arms in the United States.

(Remember what we said earlier. All international treaties, under the Supremacy Clause of our Constitution, have the force of constitutional law and may not be contradicted by state or federal legislation. The ATT would effectively repeal the Second Amendment as clearly as the Twenty-First Amendment repealed the Prohibition amendment— the Eighteenth.)

As with so many of the UN treaties, it advances under false pretenses. The nominal purpose of the ATT is to regulate the international arms trade, limiting the flow of deadly weapons across national borders to drug cartels, criminal gangs, guerillas, and organized crime (just the crowd US Attorney General Eric Holder ran guns to in the Fast and Furious operation). But the catch is that the treaty establishes an international body to promote gun control. It requires that each nation adopt regulations to limit and control export of small arms. It is easy to see how this provision would require registration and inventory of all guns in the United States and could lead to confiscation.

The *Independent Sentinel*, a publication dedicated to Second Amendment rights, notes that President Obama told Mrs. James Brady—a strong gun control advocate after her husband was shot in the Reagan assassination attempt in 1981—that the administration had not forgotten its commitment to gun control. He told her in May 2011, "I just want you to know that we are working on it. We have to go through a few processes, but under the radar."[2]

He was likely referring to the ATT.

In October 2009, Secretary of State Hillary Clinton "reversed the policies of previous presidents and stated that she would enter into talks with the international community about signing a small arms treaty."[3] And in May 2010, President Obama signaled America's willingness to negotiate such a treaty.

Hillary was quick to add that the US will insist on safeguards to protect the individual's right to bear arms, but other nations are intent on using the treaty to erode them. Debbie Hillier, Oxfam International's policy adviser (who is working on the treaty), said that "governments must resist US demands to give any single state the power to veto the treaty as this could hold the process hostage during the course of negotiations. We all on all governments to reject such a veto clause."[4]

The ATT would "tighten regulation of, and set international standards for, the import, export, and transfer of conventional weapons," according to the *Independent Sentinel*. "The treaty they are talking about," the magazine warns, "basically bans all privately-held semi-automatic weapons." Semiautomatic weapons should not be confused with machine guns. Machine guns, which are illegal in the United States, permit the rapid firing of bullets with the single pull of a trigger. A semiautomatic weapon features rapid and automatic reloading after each shot, but requires a trigger pull each time the gun is fired. One pull. One shot.

The UN gun control advocates passionately argue that "light weapons and ammunition wreaks havoc everywhere. Mobs terrorizing a neighborhood. Rebels attacking civilians or peacekeepers. Drug lords randomly killing law enforcers or anyone else interfering with their illegal businesses. Bandits hijacking humanitarian aid convoys. In all continents, uncontrolled small arms form a persisting problem."

The UN continues:

[S]mall arms are cheap, light, and easy to handle, transport and conceal. A build-up of small arms alone may not create the conflicts in which they are used, but their excessive accumulation and wide availability aggravates the tension. The violence becomes more lethal and lasts longer, and a sense of insecurity grows, which in turn lead to a greater demand for weapons.

Most present-day conflicts are fought mainly with small arms, which are broadly used in inter-State conflict. They are the weapons of choice in civil wars and for terrorism, organized crime and gang warfare.[5]

Of course, why this international trend should empower a UN agency to ban or limit US privately owned weaponry is not clear. Most nations have no right to bear arms and have made private possession illegal. As the horrific toll of international violence makes abundantly clear, these laws are not well enforced.

But, in the United States, murder is a decreasing problem. In 1993, there were 24,530 homicides in the United States.[6] Today, despite an increase in population from 250 million to 310 million, the number of homicides has dropped almost in half, to 13,756. Of these, 9,203 involved the use of a firearm.[7]

With gun violence decreasing sharply, why would we be interested in signing a global gun control treaty? The answer is clear: globalist and left-wing pressure. The liberals say that they want us to be bound by the treaty because the US is the source of 40 percent of the global arms trade.[8] But most of that is sold by the government, not by private individuals. The US, Russia, China, Israel, and Germany are the world's leading arms exporters. But the treaty is aimed at individuals, who account for a small minority of the arms traffic.

Thomas Countryman, a US assistant secretary of state, made it clear in April 2012 that the treaty is not aimed at governments. Least of all, ours. "We do not want something that would make legitimate international arms trade more cumbersome than the hurdles United States exporters already face." [9]

Those who die at the hands of such legitimate arms sales will doubtless be comforted.

GUN REGULATIONS ON THE WAY

The Treaty includes, according to the *Independent Sentinel*, "the creation of a new UN agency to regulate international weapon sales, and require countries that host firearms manufacturers to set up a compensation fund for victims of gun violence worldwide." [10]

Gun control opponents, writing in the *Independent Sentinel*, predict that,

> disguised as . . . a treaty to fight against "terrorism," "insurgency," and "international crime syndicates," the treaty would undoubtedly:
>
> 1. Enact tougher licensing requirements, making law-abiding Americans cut through even more bureaucratic red tape just to own a firearm legally;
> 2. Confiscate and destroy all "unauthorized" civilian firearms (all firearms owned by the government are excluded, of course);
> 3. Ban the trade, sale and private ownership of all semi-automatic weapons;
> 4. Create an international gun registry, setting the stage for full-scale gun confiscation. [11]

While the treaty will doubtless be filled with reassuring disclaimers, former US ambassador to the UN John Bolton has seen this kind of thing before. "After the treaty is approved and it comes into force, you will find out that it has this implication or that implication and it requires the Congress to adopt some measure that restricts ownership of firearms," he warns. "The [Obama] administration knows it cannot obtain this kind of legislation purely in a domestic context. . . . They will use an international agreement as an excuse to get domestically what they couldn't otherwise." [12]

Tom Mason, who represented the World Forum on the Future of Sports Shooting at the UN conference, said, "The treaty is a significant threat to gun owners. I think the biggest threat may be the body that would administer the treaty." [13]

The ATT sets up an Implementation Support Unit to administer its provisions. Defenders of the treaty counter that it will clearly recognize the right of individual and national self-defense and say that it will be administered by the individual nations themselves, not by the UN.

But the draft treaty provides that "parties [to the ATT] shall take all necessary measures to control brokering activities taking place within its territories . . . to prevent the diversion of exported arms into the illicit market or to unintended end users." [14]

Opponents of the treaty warn that the Implementation Support United established by the ATT will increase its own powers to make sure that nations who sign the treaty "take all necessary measures" to enforce its ban on arms trafficking. They point out that UN treaties are subject to the kind of mission creep that Ambassador Bolton warns about.

One hundred and thirty members of Congress—organized by Pennsylvania Republican congressman Mike Kelly—wrote to President Obama on July 1, 2012, to express their opposition and concern about the ATT. "The UN's actions to date indicate that the ATT is likely to pose significant threats to our national security, foreign policy, and economic interests as well as our constitutional rights," reads the letter.

"The US must establish firm red lines for the ATT and state unequivocally that it will oppose the ATT if it infringes on our rights or threatens our ability to defend our interests."[15] The congressmen demanded that the treaty exclude small arms and ammunition and recognize the right of individual self-defense.

The National Rifle Association attacked the treaty. "Any international Arms Trade Treaty (ATT) that in any way, shape or form affects the constitutional rights of American gun owners is unacceptable,"[16] Chris Cox, executive director of the NRA's Institute for Legislative Action, said in a statement. "International organizations and foreign governments do not have the right to restrict the fundamental freedoms handed down to us from our Founding Fathers."

NRA President Wayne LaPierre testified before the U.N. that "on behalf of all NRA members and American gun owners, we are here to announce that we will not tolerate any attack—from any entity or organization whatsoever—on our Constitution or on the fundamental, individual right to keep and bear arms."[17]

Ted R. Bromund, senior research fellow in the Margaret Thatcher Center for Freedom, at the Heritage Foundation, warns that the ATT is what he calls an "aspirational" treaty, meaning that it sets goals and is less specific about how to achieve them.

He warns that "Americans should realize that many of the risks to US sovereignty posed by the ATT and other aspirational treaties cannot be fully addressed by legislative action, because these risks are inherent in any effort to negotiate vague, aspirational, and universal treaties in a world full of dictatorial states. The best defense against encroachments on US sovereignty—including the ability to conduct foreign policy—rests with oversight by elected officials and the vigilance of American citizens."[18]

The combination of the aspirations of the treaty signatories to curtail small arms throughout the world and the enforcement mechanisms built into the document spell bad news for our Second Amendment freedoms if we ratify the ATT.

HILLARY'S SECRET STRATEGY FOR
IMPOSING GUN CONTROLS

NRA president Wayne LaPierre announced in July 2012 that his organization had secured the commitment of fifty-eight US Senators to oppose ratification of the Arms Trade Treaty if it contains any regulation of civilian firearms—far more than the thirty-four required to block Senate ratification. And, on July 26, 2012, fifty-one Senators said they would vote against ratification in its current form. Obama, knowing that if Hillary signed the treaty, as she had pledged to do on July 27, the day after the senatorial letter, the gun issue would become front and center in the presidential race. So the administration pulled back in a tactical retreat and the signing scheduled for that day was canceled. End of story? No way!

Here's what the play is: The United Nations General Assembly will likely approve the treaty by a two-thirds vote before election day in the US. Then the requisite sixty-five nations will sign and ratify the treaty. That sets its provisions in stone. Obama and Hillary will keep silent until after the election. Then they will sign the treaty—and Harry Reid, the Senate Majority Leader, will probably never bring it up for a vote. Knowing he would lose any ratification vote, Reid will just let the treaty take effect under the Vienna Convention—without any approval by the Senate. If President Obama is reelected, he will, of course, refuse to renounce the treaty and it will take effect without a vote of our elected representatives.

The only way to stop the treaty is to defeat Obama and/or elect a Republican Senate.

REPEAL THE REAGAN DOCTRINE

Bromund points out that the ATT is likely to mean one thing to the world's democracies but something quite different for its tyrannical dictators. He points out that many of the nations that will sign the ATT are "dictatorships. Thus, the treaty will on the one hand recognize that states such as Syria have the right to buy and sell arms and on the other hand require them to establish effective systems of import and export control that, like the current US system, consider the human rights consequences of arms transfers."

But he points out that "this is a fantasy: If a state like Syria genuinely wanted to establish such a system, the treaty would not be necessary. The ATT will effectively bind only the democracies that accept it." And, he notes, "the failure of other states to live up to their commitments under the ATT will not cause its restrictions on the US to lapse."[19]

Because the treaty is so deliberately vague, Bromund is troubled. If the treaty comes up for ratification, the Senate will find it difficult to offer informed advice and consent on the ATT because its meaning, and thus the commitments arising from it, are so poorly defined. This will also open the door for US allies with a strong commitment to multilateral institutions, left-wing non-governmental organizations, and dictatorships to pressure the US—and US businesses—to accept their interpretations of the treaty, which will seek to impinge further on US freedom of action. Finally, it will empower US officials to interpret the ATT as they see fit, which, by asking the Senate to write a blank check, raises further concerns about the effectiveness of the Senate's advice and consent role and the defense of Second Amendment freedoms.

Bromund worries that the treaty will make it impossible for the US to support freedom-loving movements throughout the world. Since the ATT will oblige signatories "not to circumvent the import control systems of other signatories," he warns that it might enable Iran to condemn the US for violating the ATT if it decided to arm Iranian rebels. The entire future of the Reagan Doctrine—the US support for human rights and pro-freedom rebellions throughout the world—might be imperiled.

Remember that it was the importation of arms to Bosnian rebels in the 1990s that held the Serbian forces at bay and reduced the carnage of their ethnic cleansing. Would the ATT stop the US from sending arms to Africa to prevent a repetition of the Rwanda massacre? Would we be obliged to respect the government of Sudan and not arm the Darfur refugees?

Writing in the *New York Post*, Heritage Foundation fellow Peter Brookes calls the idea of American participation in the ATT "foolish" and urges us to avoid it "like the plague."[20]

He points out, for example, that the treaty would likely bar the US from supplying arms to Taiwan since the UN recognizes only one Chinese government—the one in Beijing—for both the mainland and Formosa. He argues that arms shipments to Taiwan would be illegal under the treaty since the government in Taipei would technically be an insurgent entity, barred from receiving arms under the ATT.

Brookes also notes, "The treaty will also develop a list of criteria that will call upon states to keep arms out of insurgents' hands or prevent the prolonging of a conflict. Sounds nice—but what if, for instance, we find a group at some point that we want to support that is fighting an evil government? Can't do it."[21]

But then Brookes articulates the coup de grace: "[W]ho really expects state sponsors of terrorism to stop arming groups like Hamas and Hezbollah in the Middle East, the FARC in Latin America and the Taliban and the Lashkar-e-Taiba in South Asia because of a piece of paper signed at the United Nations? Come on."[22]

This treaty is one that will not stop the arms trade. It will not limit the sale by governments of arms to signatory nations. It may stop freedom forces from being able to resist tyranny in their countries. And its implementation by a UN agency—with no further Senate or congressional oversight once the president's signature is dry on the treaty—could and likely would be used to abuse, override, and limit our Second Amendment right to bear arms.

(Remember what we said earlier. All international treaties, under the Supremacy Clause of our Constitution, have the force of constitutional law and may not be contradicted by state or federal legislation. The ATT would effectively repeal the Second Amendment.)

PART THREE

UN SOVEREIGNTY AT SEA TREATY: A THIRD WORLD TAX ON AMERICA

Frustrated by the refusal of the United States and Western European nations to give them the foreign aid to which they feel entitled, the third world nations have banded together to create a vehicle to seize our wealth. They have come up with a way to intercept American and Western revenues before they even reach our treasuries and to divert them to their own needs—often directly into their autocratic rulers' bank accounts. Troubled by how difficult it is to persuade Congress to vote them money, they have decided to allocate revenue to themselves directly from our offshore oil and mineral drilling. And, once we sign the treaty, we will have nothing to say about it.

Their chosen path to our wealth is through a new Law of the Sea Treaty (known by the appropriate acronym LOST). And, believe it or not, a coalition of liberal Democrats and RINO (Republican In Name Only) senators may have the votes to get this treaty ratified.

What is extraordinary is that our own leaders are backing these efforts and our president, secretary of state, secretary of defense, and Joint Chiefs of Staff are all supporting the treaty and urging its ratification.

REAGAN AND THATCHER REJECTED THE TREATY

But not all of the world's recent leaders share their enthusiasm for the treaty. Former defense secretary Donald Rumsfeld, who recently testified against it, recounts how "thirty years ago, President Ronald Reagan asked me to meet with world leaders to represent the United States in opposition to the United Nations Law of the Sea Treaty. Our efforts soon found a persuasive supporter in British Prime Minister Margaret Thatcher."[1]

Rumsfeld recalls that when he met with Mrs. Thatcher in 1982, her conclusion on the treaty was unforgettable: "What this treaty proposes is nothing less than the international nationalization of roughly two-thirds of the Earth's surface. . . . Tell Ronnie I'm with him [in opposing the treaty]."[2]

Negotiated in the 1970s, the treaty was "presented to [Reagan] as a done deal requiring only his signature and Senate ratification. Then as now, most of the world's nations had already approved it. The Nixon, Ford and Carter administrations had all gone along. American diplomats generally supported the treaty and were shocked when Reagan changed America's policy. Puzzled by their reaction, the president was said to have responded, "But isn't that what the election was all about?"[3]

Ed Meese, who was attorney general under Reagan and who also opposes the treaty, quotes a 1978 Reagan radio address titled "Ocean Mining" in which he came out against the treaty even before he was elected. The future president said that "no national interest of ours could justify handing sovereign control of two-thirds of the Earth's surface over to the Third World."[4]

GLOBAL REDISTRIBUTION OF INCOME

The treaty fit into a growing effort by third world countries to appropriate to themselves the wealth of the developed nations.

James Malone, Reagan's point man in seeking unsuccessfully to modify the treaty, explains his president's opposition: "The treaty's provisions were intentionally designed to promote a new world order—a form of global collectivism . . . that seeks ultimately the redistribution of the world's wealth through a complex system of manipulative central economic planning and bureaucratic coercion."[5]

Doug Bandow, now a senior fellow at the Cato Institute, served as a special assistant to President Regan and a deputy representative to the Third United Nations Conference on the Law of the Sea. He bluntly explains that "the treaty would resurrect the redistributionist lobbying campaign once conducted by developing states unwilling to deal with the real causes of their economic failures. Indeed, the LOST would essentially create another UN agency with the purpose of transferring wealth from industrialized states to the Third World voting majority."[6]

In the 1970s and '80s, third world nations promoted what Bandow says they "euphemistically called the New International Economic Order—global management and redistribution of resources, technology, trade, and wealth."[7] In the United Nations, they formed a Group of seventy-seven countries that set about their search for new sources of income and wealth for their countries and their corrupt leaders. They tried to get the United Nations Industrial Development Organization (UNIDO), the United Nations Educational, Scientific and Cultural Organization (UNESCO), the Food and Agriculture Organization of the United Nations (FAO), the United Nations Centre for Transnational Corporations (CTC), the United Nations Conference on Trade and Development (UNCTAD), and the United Nations itself to help them soak rich nations to benefit their third world dictators. All these agencies "became international battlegrounds" in the third world's desperate search for wealth. Our wealth!

The demands of the third world dictators for more aid have become more insistent and their approach more militant over the past thirty years. Where once they played off the rivalry of the United States and Russia during the cold war—going first to one and then to the other in a bidding contest for their support—they now sought to play on the conscience of the developed world to pry out more aid. Suddenly music groups like U2 held concerts devoted to raising global awareness of poverty. Appeals to world compassion sparked efforts to increase foreign aid appropriations.

Britain's prime minister Tony Blair took the lead in pledging to contribute seven-tenths of one percent of his nation's Gross Domestic Product (GDP) to third world nations and called on all developed countries to follow his lead.

Global economist Jeffrey Sachs wrote a book optimistically titled

The End of Poverty, in which he chronicled the rapid decline of poverty throughout the world. Heralding China's and India's emergence from hardship, he called for massive increases in foreign aid to continue the progress so evident in east and south Asia.

But Sachs missed the point. It was not foreign aid that had lifted China and India out of poverty, but international commerce. Through private sector entrepreneurial initiative rather than public charity, these nations cut their poor populations dramatically and spread a middle-class standard of living. It was trade with the United States and direct foreign investment in their businesses rather than foreign aid that had vanquished poverty.

No matter how loudly U2 sang or Blair demanded higher levels of foreign aid, the American people weren't biting. They were largely un-moved by these appeals. While we doubled our foreign aid spending, it still comes to only four-tenths of one percent of GDP—half of the hoped-for global standard.

Seeing that the strategy of trying to shame the developed world into increased aid wasn't working, the third world dictators hit on a new vehicle to get money: the Law of the Sea Treaty.

Why not grab hold of the money that gushed out of oil wells drilled deep in the bottom of the ocean? Weren't these resources "the common heritage of mankind"? How could any nation lay claim to these rich resources that lay far off its coastline, even beyond the two-hundred-mile economic zone generally asserted by seacoast nations?

These dictatorships acted like Groucho Marx did when he learned, in his movie *Night at the Opera,* that the wealthy, elderly widow he was currently romancing had given money to the opera so they could sign a tenor who would sing for a thousand dollars a night—an astronomical sum in those days. Rubbing his hands together, Groucho said, "There's got to be some way I can get a piece of that."[8]

Bandow explains that to these African, Asian, and Latin American autocracies, "no fight was more important than that over the LOST." After all, didn't the treaty itself explicitly articulate its purpose to "contribute to the realization of a just and equitable international economic order which takes into account the interests and needs of mankind as a whole and, in particular, the special interests and needs of developing countries"?[9]

The Law of the Sea Treaty does more than just increase the flow of wealth from developed nations to third world dictatorships. It confers on them the power to tax American property.

No longer do they have to ask for money. They can demand it. And it's a lot of money. According to the US Extended Continental Shelf Task Force, which is currently mapping the undersea region, the resources there "may be worth billions if not trillions" of dollars.[10]

The treaty gives a new multinational body—the International Seabed Authority (ISA)—the right to impose taxes on offshore oil and gas wells equal to 7 percent of the royalties they would otherwise pay to their nation's treasuries. The Seabed Authority, based in Kingston, Jamaica, would rule the waves—and the seabed beneath. A body much like the United Nations' General Assembly, it is governed by 160 member nations, each with one vote.

Secretary Rumsfeld stresses that "pursuant to the treaty's Article 82, the US would be required to transfer to this entity a significant share of all royalties generated by US companies—royalties that would otherwise go to the US Treasury."[11]

"Over time, hundreds of billions of dollars could flow through the Authority with little oversight. The US would not control how those revenues are spent: The treaty empowers the Authority to redistribute these so-called international royalties to developing and landlocked nations with no role in exploring or extracting those resources."[12]

Rumsfeld calls this transfer of wealth by its real name: welfare. "This [treaty] would constitute massive global welfare, courtesy of the US taxpayer. It would be as if fishermen who exerted themselves to catch fish on the high seas were required, on the principle that those fish belonged to all people everywhere, to give a share of their take to countries that had nothing to do with their costly, dangerous and arduous efforts."[13]

US CAN'T CONTROL WHO GETS OUR MONEY

The money could go anywhere, with the US having little if any control over it. The money would go into a global fund that a thirty-six member committee of the ISA would allocate around the world. The United States would sit on the committee and have one vote, only one.

The treaty specifies that the distribution of the aid would be decided by the council based on "consensus," a provision that treaty advocates have said amounts to giving the US, in effect, a kind of veto. But experience has proven that without a formal veto the requirement of consensus would give us very little real leverage with which to direct the flow of aid, even to stop the money from going to terror-sponsoring nations or entities.

And one wonders if President Obama's representatives on the ISA Council can be counted on to fight to direct the revenue to good countries. After all, it's his administration that gives $1 billion in foreign aid to the Palestinian Authority and Hamas and $1.3 billion to the Muslim Brotherhood regime in Egypt!

Rumsfeld explains that "these sizable 'royalties' could go to corrupt dictatorships and state sponsors of terrorism. For example, as a treaty signatory and a member of the Authority's executive council, the government of Sudan—which has harbored terrorists and conducted a mass extermination campaign against its own people—would have as much say as the US on issues to be decided by the Authority." [14]

Under the treaty, the transfer of these funds does not end with nation-states. These royalty revenues would even be extended to "peoples who have not attained full independence or other self-governing status." [15] That means that groups like the Palestinian Authority and potentially other groups with terrorist ties could get in on the bounty.

The point is that it is our money, not the United Nations'. American firms prospected for the oil, financed the drilling, invented the deep-sea technology, took the risk of a dry well, and are entitled to reap the rewards of their efforts.

AIDING THIRD WORLD COUNTRIES DOESN'T HELP THEM

But, our liberal friends ask, shouldn't we extend our aid to the third world? Don't we have a moral obligation to fight poverty and help them feed their people?

But wiser heads in the developed world realize that increasing the flow of revenue to third world autocracies would just expand their opportunities for graft and corruption. The funding would not flow to their needy people but to the avaricious Swiss bank accounts.

Indeed, some economists like Dambisa Moyo, an African woman who wrote *Dead Aid: Why Aid Is Not Working and How There Is a Better Way for Africa*, believe that foreign aid is really counterproductive.

She argues that aid is just an invitation to corruption. It means that governments become like private franchises, raising their money abroad and spending it in unaccountable ways. Their citizens don't care. It's not their money. And the effort of ambitious people to get their hands on the aid sparks civil wars, coups, corruption, and political instability, which makes real economic growth impossible.

Moyo, who studied at Harvard, earned a doctorate in economics at Oxford, and worked at the World Bank, poses the challenging question: "Has more than $1 trillion in development aid to Africa over the last several decades made the African people better off?" [16]

Her answer is a resounding no. She elaborates: "In fact, across the globe the recipients of this aid are worse off; much worse off. Aid has helped make the poor poorer and growth slower. . . . The notion that aid can alleviate systemic poverty and has done so is a myth. Millions in Africa are poorer because of aid. Aid has been, and continues to be, an unmitigated political, economic, and humanitarian disaster for most parts of the developing world." [17]

Moyo says that revenues such as what the Law of the Sea would cause to flow to the third world creates a pot of money over which various factions, tribes, parties, and regions can compete. She likens it to diamond mines or oil wells, "a kind of curse because it encourages corruption and conflict, while at the same time discouraging free enterprise. Not only is aid easy to steal, as it is usually provided directly to African governments, but it also makes control over government worth fighting for. And, most importantly, the influx of aid can undermine domestic savings and investment." [18]

US foreign aid has failed in its primary mission of alleviating poverty. Since 1980, the United States has given more than $309 billion (in inflation-adjusted money) in development assistance to poor countries. (This sum does not include military aid or humanitarian relief for natural disasters.) And it hasn't worked.

Of the 97 countries that got development aid from the United States between 1980 and 2006:

- a quarter actually saw a net drop in their per capita GDP.

- 28 had almost no growth— less than one percent.

- 39 had minor growth averaging only 1–4 percent per year.

- Only 4 had real economic growth of 5 percent or more. They were Bosnia, Serbia, Cambodia, and Botswana.

WE'D HAVE TO GIVE AWAY OUR TECHNOLOGY, TOO

But sending money to third world dictators is not even the most obnoxious part of the Law of the Sea Treaty. Beyond taxing royalties, the treaty obliges American energy companies that wish to drill more than two hundred miles off our Continental Shelf to share their technologies— for free—with the ISA.

Senators Orrin Hatch (R-UT) and John Cornyn (R-TX)—both opponents of the treaty—warn that under it "nations with mining and resource recovery technologies like the United States will be obligated to share those technologies with Third World competitors, and that is one of the many issues, which trouble those of us opposed to the treaty." [19]

They add: "in other words, US companies would be forced to give away the very types of innovation that historically have made our nation a world leader while fueling our economic engine." [20]

In a phrase out of *Star Trek*, the treaty sets up an "Enterprise" to facilitate third world access to drilling technology. It provides that "if the Enterprise or developing States are unable to obtain" drilling equipment commercially, there is a duty imposed on signatory nations to "facilitate the acquisition of mining technology." [21]

Sensibly, the Cato Institute argues that "the Enterprise and developing states would find themselves unable to purchase machinery only if they were unwilling to pay the market price or were perceived as being unable to preserve trade secrets. The clause might be interpreted to mean that industrialized states, and private miners, whose 'cooperation' is to be 'ensured' by their respective governments, are then responsible for subsidizing the Enterprise's acquisition of technology." [22]

Cato also notes that the treaty empowers the Seabed Authority to "take measures . . . to promote and encourage the transfer to developing States [of] technology and scientific knowledge so that all States Parties benefit therefrom." If the US signs the treaty, the Seabed Authority would have enormous leverage over American energy companies to compel them to "share" their technology for free! [23]

American firms will have to survey the ocean floor, locate mineral reserves, raise the capital to drill, assume the risk of failure, and even pay the Enterprise a quarter-million-dollar application fee to get their approval for the well. Then, when they get oil, they must pay royalties to the Seabed Authority and give the Enterprise access to their technology!

And the application fee and royalty tax could go higher. Cato warns that the treaty allows an "as yet undetermined, level of royalties and profit sharing. The Institute notes that the 'system of payments' . . . shall be 'fair both to the contractor and to the Authority,' fees 'shall be within the range of those prevailing in respect of land-based mining of the same or similar minerals,' even though, as Cato notes, "seabed production is more expensive, riskier, and occurs in territory beyond any nation's jurisdiction."[24]

Yet some major oil companies support the treaty! They argue that their legal claims to the right to drill far offshore (beyond the two-hundred-mile limit) are shaky and that recognition of their wells by an international authority would give them the legal protection that they need.

Elliot Richardson, who led the American delegation that negotiated this treaty during the Carter years, says that the United Nations' assertion that the ocean's resources are "the common heritage of mankind" has made it impossible for any seabed mining without UN approval. He warns that "if any mining defied international law, its output would be subject to confiscation as contraband."[25]

The Cato Institute rightly asks "who would do the seizing?" There is no UN Navy, but there is a US Navy that would protect our commercial interests in the face of a hostile seizure.[26]

Indeed, Cato stresses that the arguments of the oil companies make it "all the more important that the United States refuse to ratify the [Law of the Sea Treaty]. Once Washington has done so, a future renunciation of the LOST might not be considered enough to reestablish Americans' traditional freedom on the high seas."[27]

Backers of the treaty see the agreement as a fait accompli since more than the necessary sixty nations have already ratified it, putting it into effect (according to its own terms). But, as Cato notes, "nations cannot be held to surrender their rights because other states have ratified a treaty. Put bluntly, it matters little whether or not Djibouti, Fiji, or Zambia approves of American mining consortia operating in the Pacific."[28]

SHACKLING THE US NAVY

The Law of the Sea Treaty has other horrific implications. Essentially, it makes the entire seabed and the waters above it the sovereign property of the United Nations and disempowers the US Navy.

Ever since the United States won the Cold War and acquired un-questioned global military superiority, the other nations of the world have sought to rein in American force. Two treaties represent their most audacious effort to stop the United States from exercising its military sway throughout the world.

The Law of the Sea Treaty gives the International Seabed Authority (ISA) the right to adjudicate disputes over the seas, deciding who can sail where and drill where on the seabed. Currently, the US Navy, as a practical matter, makes these determinations since no one can challenge its power. But prevailing anti-American sentiment throughout the world is leading other nations to try to reduce its power.

The second effort to restrain our military power is through the International Criminal Court. It would ban any American president—on possible penalty of criminal prosecution before the court—from going to war without the approval of the UN Security Council, a body hobbled by the Russian and Chinese veto power. The treaty would, in effect, require the approval of Moscow and Beijing before our armed forces could be committed to combat. (See more on the ICC in Part Six.)

The right of open seas and freedom of navigation is maintained for all nations by the unrivaled and unequaled power of the US Navy, which, after Great Britain found its resources too limited to afford a large navy, has protected open seas for almost a hundred years.

But, now, in an era of defense spending cuts, some urge that the US Navy pull back from its historic mission and turn the protection of free navigation over to the International Seabed Authority.

Disputes that were once adjudicated by the US Navy will now go before international arbitrators meeting in Hamburg, Germany, appointed by the ISA—and almost certainly hostile to American interests. The arbitrators, whose decisions are binding on signatory nations, are chosen by the parties to the dispute, each getting the right to name one or two of the five judges. In the event that a fifth judge satisfactory to the contending nations could not be negotiated, the power to appoint the judges would fall on the secretary-general of the United Nations, Ban Ki-moon, whose tenure has been noted for its corruption, anti-Americanism, and overt advocacy of the transfer of resources to the third world. Good luck getting a fair trial out of him!

Peter Brookes of the Heritage Foundation asks the key question: "Why risk sacrificing US sovereignty under the treaty if it makes us no more secure? After all, what initially established and still ensures freedom of navigation under international law is naval power. To secure navigational freedom, territorial rights and all national and international interests addressed in LOST, we must maintain the strength of the US Navy, not look to an anachronistic pact that is intent on advancing a one-world agenda."[29]

The treaty itself has been kicking around for years. Negotiated by the misguided globalists of the Carter administration, the drive for US participation was only temporarily halted after Reagan refused to sign on in 1982.

President Clinton signed the treaty Reagan had rejected, after it was renegotiated in 1994. The changed treaty was hailed as solving all the objections Reagan had raised and Clinton called for prompt Senate ratification. But a careful examination of these changes revealed that they were largely cosmetic, fudging some issues and avoiding others. Those who had opposed the treaty are largely still opposed. Conservative objections to the revised document were so strong that the Republican majority on the Senate Foreign Affairs Committee refused to report the treaty to the floor of the Senate in the 1990s.

Now, in the current drive for ratification, Secretary of State Hillary Clinton mocked those who raised legitimate questions about the treaty in her Senate testimony, saying that the arguments against the treaty "cannot even be taken with a straight face." She said the opposition to the treaty was "based in ideology and mythology, not in facts, evidence, or the consequences of our continuing failure to accede to the treaty."[30]

As noted, the secretary of state dismissed concerns over the treaty, noting that if the US signed it or any UN treaty, "[o]f course, that means the black helicopters are on their way,"[31] a reference to conspiracy theories about a world government and a quote that inspired the title of this book. Thank you, Hillary!

One of the changes made in 1994 excluded military vessels from the regulation of the International Seabed Authority. But Senator James Inhofe (R-OK) notes that while

> proponents say the treaty exempts military activity from international litigation, those of us opposing it are deeply concerned because this terribly flawed document fails to define what is included in that exemption. In addition, it opens the US military to the jurisdiction of international courts and governing bodies.

The Senator noted that "military training exercises that do not have the approval of other nations could be prevented because of potentially negative environmental impacts. US military vessels could be stopped on the grounds that they are too heavy a polluter.[32]

Currently, the US Navy is subject to the Inter-Governmental Maritime Consultative Organization, now called the International Maritime Organization (IMO). The IMO sets maritime laws to improve safety at sea, facilitate trade, and protect the marine environment. The Law of the Sea Treaty would supersede the IMO. The IMO already gives the US a free hand to pursue commerce and military operations around the globe. So why hamper and hinder our own Navy and subject us to the jurisdiction of the Seabed Authority?

CAN THE TREATY STOP CHINA AND RUSSIA FROM THEIR TERRITORIAL CLAIMS?

Defenders of the Law of the Sea Treaty say that it is necessary to resolve two regional problems: China's attempt to assert control over the South China Sea and Russia's efforts to claim sovereignty over the Arctic ice shelf, where the warming global climate may make oil drilling more technically feasible in the future.

China is a signatory to the Law of the Sea Treaty but, nevertheless, it is ignoring one of its key provisions—the offshore exclusive economic zone. The treaty gives each country bordering the ocean a zone of two hundred miles off its coast in which it can drill for oil or engage in any economic activity. Even though the treaty bars other nations from economic activity—such as oil drilling—within another country's two-hundred-mile zone, China is claiming that it can drill anywhere in the South China Sea, even right off the Vietnam coast.

In June 2012, the China National Offshore Oil Corporation announced that it was "offering a new batch of oil-exploration blocks inside the 200-nautical mile exclusive economic zone granted to Vietnam under the United Nations' Law of the Sea Treaty."[33]

Vietnam protested, but the International Seabed Authority—charged with enforcing the treaty—did nothing to bar the Chinese action. China does whatever it wants, wherever it wants, as usual, and only nations like the United States scrupulously abide by their treaty commitments.

To believe that China would be deterred from its imperialistic ambitions by the rulings of the International Seabed Authority is ridiculous. The fact that China is already a signatory to the treaty has obviously not stopped it from trying to elbow aside not only Vietnam, but also the Philippines, Malaysia, and Indonesia for control of the South China Sea.

Peter Brookes debunks the idea that the treaty would inhibit China, noting that China, "claims 'indisputable sovereignty' over the entire South China Sea—more than 1 million square miles. (LOST allows for 12-mile territorial waters and a 200-mile Exclusive Economic Zone—or EEZ—from a country's coastline.) Beijing has flouted LOST for years while building a mighty military machine, especially a navy, to assert its claims. It's fantasy believing that an American signature on a piece of paper will change China's mind about the South China Sea and EEZ freedom of navigation."[34]

One of the nation's most astute observers of China, Gordon Chang, agrees. Writing in the *World Affairs Journal,* Chang said that "although Beijing ratified the [LOST] pact in June 1996, it continues to issue maps claiming the entire South China Sea. That claim is, among other things, incompatible with the treaty's rules. It's no wonder Beijing notified the UN in 2006 that it would not accept international arbitration of its sovereignty claims." [35]

China seems totally undaunted by its treaty commitment under the Law of the Sea Treaty.

Nor would LOST be any more helpful in adjudicating the controversy with Russia over the Arctic.

Brookes points out that advocates of the treaty say we

supposedly need to be inside the LOST "tent" to counter Moscow's and others' claims in the Arctic, where climate change might allow harvesting of once-inaccessible natural resources around the North Pole. (US government surveys suggest about one-third of the world's yet-to-be-discovered, recoverable natural resources are below Arctic ice floes.)

In fact, we're already a member of the Arctic Ocean Conference— which is doing a good job of resolving the claims by the five circumpolar states (the United States, Canada, Russia, Denmark and Norway) in the High North. [36]

Former assistant secretary of defense Frank Gaffney points out that it is a lot easier to get five governments to agree than the 160 that make up the International Seabed Authority. [37]

And all this assumes that the Seabed Authority would dispense justice. The record of the United Nations is dismal in this regard and the chances are that the ISA nations would seek to curry favor with Moscow or Beijing—or repay their bribes and favors—by unjust and arbitrary rulings, even if just to stick it to the United States.

Defense Secretary Leon Panetta defended the treaty before the Senate Foreign Relations Committee, saying that "by moving off the sidelines, by sitting at the table of nations that have acceded to this treaty, we can defend our interests, we can lead the discussions, we will be able to influence those treaty bodies that develop and interpret the Law of the Sea." [38]

But Frank Gaffney argues, "This is simply not so if, as is true of the LOST's various institutions, we would have but one seat among many, and no certainty that we can decisively 'influence bodies that develop and interpret the law of the sea.' " [39]

"In fact," Gaffney adds, "thanks to the rigged-game nature of those institutions, such bodies can be relied upon to hamstring us—by, for example, applying environmental regulations over which we have no control to our Navy's anti-submarine warfare exercises and our domestic emissions into inland air and water that migrates to the international oceans." [40]

TREATY OPENS DOOR TO NAVAL WEAKNESS

Yet admirals and Navy service chiefs have advocated ratifying the Law of the Sea Treaty. General Martin Dempsey, chairman of the Joint Chiefs of Staff, for example, said this treaty "codifies navigational rights and freedoms essential for our global mobility." [41]

Former defense secretary Rumsfeld rejects the Navy's argument for the treaty:

The most persuasive argument for the treaty is the US Navy's desire to shore up international navigation rights. It is true that the treaty might produce some benefits, clarifying some principles and perhaps making it easier to resolve certain disputes. But our Navy has done quite well without this treaty for the past 200 years, relying often on centuries-old, well-established customary international law to assert navigational rights. Ultimately, it is our naval power that protects international freedom of navigation. This treaty would not make a large enough additional contribution to counterbalance the problems it would create. [42]

Senator James Inhofe (R-OK) argues that "ceding any authority to an international body is not only a threat to our sovereignty, it also creates another avenue for other nations to stop US unilateral activity."[43]

So why are the admirals pushing the treaty? Inhofe believes that the likely future weakness of the US Navy may be at play here. He explains that "some fear the Navy is at a tipping point. Increased global threats, combined with fewer resources, have created growing concern for its future. Devastating budget cuts under the Obama administration mean doing even more with much less. If the proposed defense cuts through sequestration go into effect, potential cuts include the littoral combat ship, amphibious ships, a reduction in aircraft carriers and far fewer sailors. After sequestration, our fleet could be smaller than 230 ships—the smallest since 1915."[44]

Inhofe wonders, "could it be that some have decided to put their hope in a piece of paper rather than provide the resources necessary to maintain our Navy's traditional strength?"[45]

But it is pure fantasy to assume that the Seabed Authority would be impartial and just in its rulings. And it is further fantasy to believe that powers like Russia and China would listen to it. What recourse would we have if they don't? Both nations have veto power in the UN Security Council and can stop any enforcement action with teeth. The US will, of course, honor the decisions of the authority if we join, but other, autocratic nations will thumb their noses at it.

Brookes says that relying on the treaty rather than on our own Navy to keep the sea-lanes open is "outsourcing national security"![46]

Democratic Senator Chris Coons (D-DE) asked General Dempsey the key question during hearings on the LOST: "Does failure to ratify this treaty . . . in any way compromise the ability of the United States to project force around the world, to support and sustain our allies . . . ? Are we at risk as a result of failure to ratify this treaty?"

Dempsey's response boiled down to "no."[47]

"Our ability to project force will not deteriorate," he said, if we refrain from ratifying the treaty.[48]

A BACKDOOR GLOBAL WARMING TREATY

In 1997, amid much fanfare, the nations of the world signed the Kyoto Protocol on Global Climate Change. The treaty took effect in 2005. While it was signed and ratified by 191 nations, the United States, to the intense frustration of the global community, never approved it. Indeed, it has never even been submitted to the Senate for ratification, so slight would be its chances. (In 2011, Canada renounced the treaty.)

The document commits thirty-seven largely European and Western nations to a 5 percent reduction in greenhouse gas emissions. While the US did not ratify the treaty, the fact is that we have more than doubled the reduction goals of the treaty through market forces—high gasoline and low natural gas prices—and public education and conservation. China, India, and much of the developing world refused to sign up for any carbon emission reductions and have not achieved any. For more information about the US record on curbing carbon emissions, see the chapter on Saudi Arabia in our previous book, *Screwed!*.

But it has been a goal of the liberal globalists to get Uncle Sam's signature on a global climate change treaty. They say that this is because the US generates one-quarter of the world's greenhouse gases. But America's record in cutting emissions is so extraordinary that it gives the lie to this stated objective. Their real goal is to control the United States, diminish our power, and assert regulatory jurisdiction over our power plants, factories, and entire economy.

Obama tried to force our cooperation in this effort by pushing Congress to enter a global system of cap and trade that obliged us to pay for our emissions by giving money to third world nations that do not emit comparable levels of greenhouse gas. His bill passed Nancy Pelosi's House but was rejected by the Senate (even when the Democrats had the requisite sixty votes to pass it if they wanted to do so).

So when Congress didn't act as Obama wanted, he turned his attention to the Law of the Sea Treaty. Environmentalists hope that they can bind the US finally to their emission targets by getting us to ratify the treaty.

How does LOST replace the Kyoto accords? It requires its signatories to prevent the release of pollution from land-based sources that can enter the ocean through either the atmosphere or from seagoing vessels.

Article 212 of the treaty states, in part, "States shall adopt laws and regulations to prevent, reduce and control pollution of the marine environment from or through the atmosphere. . . . States, acting especially through competent international organizations . . . shall endeavor to establish global and regional rules, standards and recommended practices and procedures to prevent, reduce and control pollution." [49]

When it was written in the 1970s, nobody was thinking about climate change. But today, green advocates are breathlessly awaiting Senate ratification of LOST so they can use this provision to force emissions controls on American power plants and industries.

Environmentalists claim that carbon dioxide emissions into the atmosphere create global warming through what they call the "greenhouse effect." And, conversely, the warmer the ocean becomes, the more it emits carbon dioxide on its own. The ocean, literally, pollutes itself!

At the Senate hearing on LOST in June 2008, Fred Smith, president of the Competitive Enterprise Institute, said that he believed that the UN will "look upstream" at the causes of marine pollution and pass binding regulations on signatory nations to reduce them. [50]

Already, environmentalists have begun an action under LOST to stop the United Kingdom from operating its power plant at Sellafield, which produces MOX nuclear fuel for Japan's reactors. Sellafield has closed anyway after the Fukayama nuclear power plant disaster. But the precedent has been set that LOST can be used to modify the environmental policies of signatory nations. (The UK is a signatory.) [51]

The latest panic among environmentalists concerns the "acidification" of the ocean. About a quarter of atmospheric carbon dioxide goes into the ocean, where it forms carbonic acid and changes the base/acidic ratio (pH ratio) of the seas.

Between 1740 and 1994, scientists tell us that surface ocean pH has dropped from 8.25 to 8.14, almost a 30 percent increase in the acidity of the oceans. Environmentalists worry that the change in pH may impact our food supply from the seas.

Christopher C. Horner, writing in the *Wall Street Journal*, says that "LOST is a sweeping regime cracking down on all activities arguably depositing pollutants into the seas. Under the precautionary principle, which LOST adopts, allegation is sufficient to establish the offense. With 'ocean acidification' the latest nominee to supplant troubled CO_2-warming theory, LOST supplants the failed Kyoto Treaty. It invites attacks on, e.g., America's transport and energy policies, claiming our cars and coal-fired power plants contribute to the latest claimed phenomenon, 'acidification.'"[52]

WILL THE SENATE RATIFY LOST?

The fact that the Senate is even considering ratifying LOST is hard to fathom. Why would we subject ourselves to the jurisdiction of a third world–dominated body that hates us?

As Gaffney says: "If Americans have learned anything about the United Nations over the last 50 years, it is that this 'world body' is, at best, riddled with corruption and incompetence. At worst, its bureaucracy, agencies and members are overwhelmingly hostile to the United States and other freedom-loving nations, most especially Israel."[53]

Michelle Malkin asks the key question: "So why on earth would the United States Senate possibly consider putting the UN on steroids by assenting to its control of seven-tenths of the world's surface?"[54]

After all, let's remember with whom we are dealing when we give the United Nations the kind of power conferred by LOST. Malkin lists the "well-documented fiascoes" that bespeckle the UN's history, including "the UN-administered Iraq Oil-for-Food program; investigations and cover-ups of corrupt practices at the organization's highest levels; child sex-slave operations and rape squads run by UN peacekeepers; and the absurd, yet relentless, assault on alleged Israeli abuses of human rights by majorities led by despotic regimes in Iran, Cuba, Syria and Libya." [55]

She fittingly warns that "the predictable effect of US accession to the UN Convention on the Law of the Sea—better known as the Law of the Sea Treaty (or LOST)—would be to transform the UN from a nuisance and laughingstock into a world government: The United States would confer upon a UN agency called the International Seabed Authority (IA) the right to dictate what is done on, in and under the world's oceans. Doing so, America would become party to surrender of immense resources of the seas and what lies beneath them to the dictates of unaccountable, nontransparent multinational organizations, tribunals and bureaucrats." [56]

This does not sound good.

So what will the Senate do?

In plotting how to get approval for this act of self-enslavement, the Obama administration has craftily decided to seek ratification only during the lame-duck session of the Senate, after the ballots have been counted in the 2012 election. Then, some senators will be retiring— a few voluntarily and a great many Democrats involuntarily—and they will have no worries about running for reelection. For the others, the classes that will face reelection in 2014 and 2016, the balloting is in the distant future and not a matter of immediate concern.

Obama's hope is that these factors induce senators to back him in passing the treaty. He used much the same tactics in getting the START Treaty with Russia ratified, submitting it to the lame-duck session of the Senate after the massacre of 2010 had left many senators still in office but doomed to retirement as soon as the new year dawned. This one-sided giveaway to Russia—which limited ballistic and strategic nuclear weapons but did nothing to curb the tactical nuclear weapons in which Moscow has a decided advantage—was ratified easily by the lame-duck body.

Likely all Democratic senators will back the treaty. But since a two-thirds majority is needed, the support of 14 Republicans, in addition to all 53 Democrats, will be required for ratification. With 47 Republicans in the current Senate, if 34 vote no, the treaty can be scuttled.

By a razor-thin margin, the Republicans in the Senate seem to be coming through. In July of this year, the bare minimum thirty-four Republican senators signed a letter to Majority Leader Harry Reid signaling their intention to vote against the treaty. Is the treaty dead? Not by a long shot! Several of the thirty-four senators only jumped on board the bandwagon at the end and expressed doubts about voting no. Most important, at this writing, the two top Republicans on the Foreign Affairs Committee in the Senate—Dick Lugar (R-IN) and Bob Corker (R-TN)—weren't among the thirty-four opponents. Lugar, the ranking Republican on the Committee, supports the treaty, and Corker, the likely incoming chairman should the Republicans win the Senate (Lugar was defeated in a primary), is uncommitted. We need to keep up the pressure to make sure these folks stay committed to vote no.

Their letter began: "We are writing to let you know that we believe this Convention reflects political, economic, and ideological assumptions which are inconsistent with American values and sovereignty." [57]

The Republicans laid out their reasons: "by its current terms, the Law of the Sea Convention encompasses economic and technology interests in the deep sea, redistribution of wealth from developed to undeveloped nations, freedom of navigation in the deep sea and exclusive economic zones which may impact maritime security, and environmental regulation over virtually all sources of pollution." [58]

They particularly highlighted their concerns about the cessation of sovereignty to the United Nations. "To effect the treaty's broad regime of governance," they wrote, "we are particularly concerned that United States sovereignty could be subjugated in many areas to a supranational government that is chartered by the United Nations under the 1982 Convention. Further, we are troubled that compulsory dispute resolution could pertain to public and private activities including law enforcement, maritime security, business operations, and nonmilitary activities performed aboard military vessels." [59]

They concluded flatly by saying, "If this treaty comes to the floor, we will oppose its ratification." [60]

Bravo!

Here's the list of the Republicans who signed the letter:

Jon Kyl (R-AZ)	Jeff Sessions (R-AL)
Jim Inhofe (R-OK)	Mike Crapo (R-ID)
Roy Blunt (R-MO)	Orrin Hatch (R-UT)
Pat Roberts (R-KS)	John Barrasso (R-WY)
David Vitter (R-LA)	Richard Shelby (R-AL)
Ron Johnson (R-WI)	John Thune (R-SD)
John Cornyn (R-TX)	Richard Burr (R-NC)
Jim DeMint (R-SC)	Saxby Chambliss (R-GA)
Tom Coburn (R-OK)	Dan Coats (R-IN)
John Boozman (R-AK)	John Hoeven (R-ND)
Rand Paul (R-KY)	Roger Wicker (R-MS)
Ron Portman (R-OH)	Marco Rubio (R-FL)
Kelly Ayotte (R-NH)	Chuck Grassley (R-IA)
Mike Johanns (R-NE)	Jim Moran (R-KS)
Johnny Isakson (R-GA)	Mitch McConnell (R-KY)
Jim Risch (R-ID)	Pat Toomey (R-PA)
Mike Lee (R-UT)	Dean Heller (R-NV) [61]

But what we really need to focus on is the ones who did *not* affix their signatures.

Senators John McCain (R-AZ) and Dick Lugar (R-IN) have publicly endorsed the treaty. That leaves these senators as uncommitted:

Bob Corker (R-TN)

Lindsay Graham (R-SC)

Lamar Alexander (R-TN)

Thad Cochran (R-MS)

Kay Bailey Hutchison (R-TX)

Lisa Murkowski (R-AK)

Scott Brown (R-MA)

Olympia Snowe (R-ME)

Susan Collins (R-ME)

Likely RINOs (Republicans in Name Only) Snowe and Collins of Maine are going to back the treaty, all the more so since Snowe is retiring.

A bunch of senators from conservative southern states—Alexander (TN), Cochran (MS), Graham (SC), and Hutchison (TX, but retiring)—may be subject to pressure.

Murkowski from Alaska might feel she needs to vote for the treaty because of her worry about Russian Arctic claims. But can she be deluded enough to think that the UN would rule in our favor?

Scott Brown of Massachusetts comes from a liberal northern state and it will be harder for him to vote no, but he's a man of deep conservative convictions and well might stand up for American sovereignty.

But the larger point is that the ball is in our court. It is not Blue Dog Democrats we must persuade but Republicans who trumpet their conservatism. It is within the Red States and among the Red Senators that we must find courageous members willing to vote no.

If you live in one of the states where these senators are from, *go to work*! Our sovereignty depends on it!

PART FOUR

THE UN TRIES TO REGULATE THE INTERNET

Authoritarian regimes throughout the world, including China, Russia, Iran, and the Arab nations, are trying to hijack an obscure UN agency, the International Telecommunication Union (ITU), to take over the Internet and give them the power to regulate its content and restrict its usage.

And the mainstream media—with the exception of the *Wall Street Journal*—has yet to cover it (as of July 2012, when this is being written).

The world's dictators realized long ago that their power rested, ultimately, on their ability to control the flow of information to their peoples. Joseph Goebbels, Hitler's propaganda minister, pioneered the "big lie" in assuring the Führer of continuing popular support. Now, facing the challenge of the free flow of information over the Internet, the world's authoritarian regimes have spent billions trying to censor the flow of information to their citizens.

Reuters explains how China "has developed the world's most advanced censorship and surveillance system" to police Internet activity in an effort to restrict the information flow to its 485 million Web users.[1]

The news service notes that "the Chinese model is spreading to other authoritarian regimes. And governments worldwide . . . are aggressively trying to legislate the Internet."[2]

To understand the lengths to which Beijing will go to stop the free flow of information on the Internet, let's remember that on the twenty-fifth anniversary of the Tiananmen Square uprising, Chinese censors prevented the search for specific words connected to the massacre of students. Anything to keep things quiet.

Now these dictatorial regimes have hit on a new solution: United Nations regulation and control of the Internet.

Their chosen instrument of control, the ITU, was set up in 1865 to regulate the telegraph and was brought into the United Nations in the modern era. In 1988, the member nations of the ITU adopted International Telecommunication Regulations, which deregulated much of the industry. These days, this quaint nineteenth-century agency stays in business to regulate long-distance phone calls and satellite orbits.

PUTIN FINDS HIS INTERNET COMMISSAR

Then, Russia's strongman Vladimir Putin had an idea: Use the ITU to regulate the Internet. Stop that pesky free flow of information and data that arms his domestic critics and stop his dissidents from using the Net to communicate their plans to resist his autocracy. He met with the secretary-general of the ITU, Hamadoun Touré, in June 2011. At the meeting "Putin commended a proposal from Touré for 'establishing international control over the Internet using the monitoring and supervisory capabilities of the International Telecommunication Union (ITU).'"[3] Turning vocabulary on its head, the Russian ruler said, "if we are going to talk about democratization of international relations, I think a critical sphere is information exchange and global control over such exchange."[4] He did not explain how controlling information would promote "democratization."

Putin shopped his proposal to his friends in China, who have worked ever since to line up support for crippling the Internet. The deed is to be done at the World Conference on International Telecommunications to be held in Dubai in December 2012. Russia, China, Iran, and others of the world's worst countries are planning to use the forum to push through a new treaty expanding the powers of the ITU and, through it, their ability to silence the Internet and make it conform to their political agenda and to bring the Internet under the regulatory thumb of the United Nations.

Touré, a native of Mali in Africa, is the ideal person to suit Putin's objectives. If ever Putin found the right man for the job of controlling the Internet, Touré is it. He studied at the Technical Institute of Electronics and Telecommunication of—get this—Leningrad, receiving a master's degree in electrical engineering, and a PhD from the Moscow Technical University of Communications and Informatics.[5]

Leningrad, now St. Petersburg, is, of course, Putin's original stomping ground. Touré's Russian educational background may help to explain his receptivity to Putin's proposals.

And a rebuttable presumption would indicate that Hamadoun Touré was—and perhaps still is—a communist. Born in 1953, he would have been educated in the Soviet Union during the 1970s and early '80s when the nation was under the rule of Party Secretary Leonid Brezhnev. No glasnost reformer he. Brezhnev kept the USSR under iron communist rule until Mikhail Gorbachev broke open the nation's politics.

Why would a young man from Mali want to be schooled in Russia? And, more important, why would communist Russia want him? And why would Soviet Russia help him acquire expertise in telecommunications, electronics, and "informatics"? We can only speculate, but the thought is not comforting.

Putin found his man!

And Touré is the person the UN would pick to be its Internet commissar—er, coordinator!

Never mind that the open, deregulated Internet has been the font of global creativity and innovation. Its free speech is politically inconvenient for Russia, China, Iran, and other third world dictatorships. Josh Peterson of the *Daily Caller* writes that "while many US policymakers and industry analysts agree that . . . deregulation is the reason why growth and innovation has been so explosive on the Internet in the past several decades, an international movement wants to give international governing bodies more power to police the Internet."[6]

NEGOTIATIONS ARE SECRET

The negotiators who are drawing up the plan for Internet regulation—including the delegates from the United States—have been keeping their plans top secret as they prepare their proposals for presentation to the Dubai Conference. There all 193 UN member countries will meet to discuss and possibly adopt their proposal. Each nation has one vote and none will have a veto. The *Wall Street Journal* warns that the authoritarian nations pushing for Internet regulation "could use the International Telecommunications Regulations to take control of the Internet."[7]

Particularly chilling is the ease with which the UN could assume the power to regulate the Internet. All the would-be regulators need is a majority vote at the Dubai Conference. *Journal* reporter Gordon Crovitz warns: "It may be hard for the billions of Web users or the optimists of Silicon Valley to believe that an obscure agency of the UN can threaten their Internet, but authoritarian regimes are busy lobbying a majority of the UN members to vote their way."[8]

The proposal for Internet regulation has been gaining supporters outside of just the group of authoritarian countries that are pushing for its adoption. Brazil and India, for example, have joined Russia and China in backing aspects of the proposal. Together these four nations comprise the BRIC group (Brazil, Russia, India, and China), which is often poised as a counterweight to the power of the US and the European Union. Vinton Cerf commented that "Brazil and India have surprised me with their interest in intervening and vying for control [over the Internet]."[9]

Otherwise, Cerf noted that support for ITU regulation of the Net came from countries like Syria and Saudi Arabia, "who are threatened by openness and freedom of expression." He said these countries "are most interested in gaining control [over the Internet] through this treaty."[10] It has not escaped the notice of the dictators and monarchs who rule these countries that the Internet and social media played key roles in the Arab Spring revolutions of recent years.

Under the one-nation, one-vote rules of the ITU, technologically backward and tiny countries can literally force the rest of the world to submit to regulation of the Internet! And don't discount the very real possibility that Russian and Chinese leaders are working overtime to buy the votes of African, Latin American, Asian, and Oceanian nations. These countries, often with only very small Internet user populations, may have no stake in preserving Internet freedom and may be willing to sell it out for some financial reward (either to their countries or to themselves personally).

And what a welcome move Internet regulation would be for the petty tyrants and strongmen who rule most of Africa! The pesky revolutions and civil wars could be nipped in the bud by Internet controls. How happy they would be to rein in free speech so they can rule—and plunder—their populations in peace.

(See Part Ten in this book on the status of global freedom to understand how tyrants and dictators constitute a majority of the membership of the UN.)

All this has led Cerf, one of the founders of the Web and currently a vice president of Google, to tell Congress recently that these proposals for regulation mean "the open Internet has never been at higher risk than it is now." [11]

Cerf warned, "If all of us do not pay attention to what's going on, users worldwide will be at risk of losing the open and free Internet that has brought so much to so many." [12]

Cerf said the implications of the potential treaty regulating the Internet are "potentially disastrous." He added that more international control over the Net could trigger a "race to the bottom" to restrict Internet freedom, "choking innovation and hurting American business abroad." [13]

Richard Grenell, who served as spokesman and adviser to four US ambassadors to the UN between 2001 and 2009, said that "having the UN or any international community regulate the Internet only means you're going to have the lowest common denominator of 193 countries." [14]

We would not know of this plan to squelch Internet freedom but for a courageous—and still anonymous—leaker who unveiled a 212-page planning document that Crovitz, writing in the *Wall Street Journal*, reports is "being used by governments to prepare for the December conference."

The leak materialized when Jerry Brito and Eli Dourado, George Mason University researchers, frustrated by the secrecy of the talks, created a website called WCITLeaks.org and invited anyone with access to documents outlining the UN proposals to post them online "to foster greater transparency." [15]

That those who would protect the freedom of the Internet had to go to such lengths to find out what is being contemplated is itself a scandal. Why on earth would the delegates from the United States and the European democracies consent to secret negotiations and allow the documents and proposals being distributed to be shielded from public view or scrutiny? These talks do not concern top-secret military or intelligence matters. There is no valid reason for having kept them secret. But the fact that the Western delegates consented to the gag order indicates how supinely they are confronting this threat to freedom.

Of course, the autocratic nations want to negotiate to squelch the Internet in secret. Secrecy for the likes of the rulers in Moscow, Beijing, and Tehran is the norm. The last thing they would want is for their own people to know of their efforts to keep the truth from them. And, these tyrants must realize that exposure of their plans would help to doom them. (That's why we wrote this book!)

Dourado—one of the two courageous men who facilitated the leak—explained that "these proposals show that many ITU member states want to use international agreements to regulate the Internet by crowding out bottom-up institutions, imposing charges for international communication, and controlling the content that consumers can access online." [16]

Crovitz, one of the only journalists covering this horrific development, notes that "the broadest proposal in the draft materials is an initiative by China to give countries authority over 'the information and communication infrastructure within their state' and require that online companies 'operating in their territory' use the Internet 'in a rational way'—in short, to legitimize full government control." [17]

The Internet Society, which represents the engineers around the world who keep the Internet functioning, says this proposal "would require member states to take on a very active and inappropriate role in patrolling" the Internet.[18]

Crovitz reports other proposals in the planning document:

- "Give the UN power to regulate online content for the first time, under the guise of protecting against computer malware or spam.

- "Russia and some Arab countries want to be able to inspect private communications such as email.

- "Russia and Iran propose new rules to measure Internet traffic along national borders and bill the originator of the traffic, as with international phone calls. That would result in new fees to local governments and less access to traffic from US 'originating' companies such as Google, Facebook and Apple. A similar idea has the support of European telecommunications companies, even though the Internet's global packet switching makes national tolls an anachronistic idea.

- "Another proposal would give the UN authority over allocating Internet addresses. It would replace Icann [Internet Corporation for Assigned Names and Numbers], the self-regulating body that helped ensure the stability of the Internet, under a contract from the US Commerce Department." [19] Currently, nongovernmental institutions, including ICANN, oversees the Web's management and its technical standards.

The Russian and Chinese justification for Internet censorship—that it would fight hacking (at which they are the world's masters)—is specious. Congressmen Michael McCaul (R-TX) and Jim Langevin (D-RI), the cochairs of the Congressional Cybersecurity Caucus, note that "[i]t must be made clear that efforts to secure the Internet against malicious hacking do not need to interfere with this freedom and the United States will oppose any attempt to blur the line between the two." [20]

China's stated rationale for its efforts to regulate the Internet is preposterous. The tyrants of Beijing say that their proposal "raises a series of basic principles of maintaining information and network security which cover the political, military, economic, social, cultural, technical and other aspects." The government statement continued: "The principles stipulate that countries shall not use such information and telecom technologies to conduct hostile behaviors and acts of aggression or to threaten international peace and security and stress that countries have the rights and obligations to protect their information and cyberspace as well as key information and network infrastructure from threats, interference, and sabotage attacks." [21]

This statement comes from the government that, more than any other, tries to interfere with and sabotage the Internet. Beijing employs tens of thousands of specially trained hackers whose job is to pry loose military and technological secrets from American and European governments and companies. Now this Internet pirate-regime is calling for greater "security"!

But the reality, of course, is that the only "hostile behavior" or "act of aggression" that is likely to invade Chinese cyberspace is the truth. Facts, accurate reporting, correct data, and public debate are the only acts of aggression China is trying to regulate. Indeed, China wants the ITU to collect IP addresses of Internet users so it can identify dissidents, whom it will move to suppress.

AMERICA SEEMS TO BE ACQUIESCING

As you are reading these outrageous proposals, you are probably saying to yourself what we said when we first saw them—that the United States and the European Union would never permit these changes and regulations to take effect.

But not so fast. Crovitz reports that while the leaked documents suggest that US negotiators are objecting to the regulatory changes behind closed doors, they are doing so "politely." [22]

Very politely. Apparently, the US called the Chinese proposals for Internet control "both unnecessary and beyond the appropriate scope" of UN regulation. Then, to soften the blow, the leaked document notes that "the US looks forward to a further explanation from China with regard to the proposed amendments, and we note that we may have further reaction at that time." [23]

American delegates also objected to proposals to give the ITU a role in regulating Internet content, tamely noting that they do "not believe" the ITU can play such a role.

Crovitz writes that the American objections are "weak responses even by Obama administration standards." [24]

From Washington, the Obama administration's response to the Internet governance proposals has been muted and laggard. Ambassador Phil Verveer, deputy assistant secretary of state for international communications and information policy, noted that some of the pending proposals, if adopted, "could limit the Internet as an open and innovative platform by potentially allowing governments to monitor and restrict content or impose economic costs upon international data flows." [25]

But, in the next breath, he denied that any of the pending proposals would give the ITU "direct Internet governance authority." [26]

Verveer's circumspection in attacking the regulatory proposals— and his use of wording such as "could limit" and "potentially allow"— indicates less than hard and fast opposition. And the administration's willingness to keep secret the negotiations themselves suggests that Hillary Clinton's State Department and Barack Obama's White House may be slender reeds to rely on in keeping the Internet open and free.

Both Secretary of State Clinton and President Obama owe us an explanation of why they countenanced secrecy in these negotiations during which our free speech is on the line!

Indeed, as of this writing, the only statement from the administration on the possible UN Internet controls came from a May 2, 2012, blog entry by the White House's Office of Science and Technology Policy, which read: "Centralized control [of the Internet] would threaten the ability of the world's citizens to freely connect and express themselves by placing decision-making power in the hands of global leaders who have demonstrated a clear lack of respect for the right of free speech."[27]

Again, what is worrying is the muted nature of the administration's objections. So radical a proposal as to put the Internet under UN control and to give Russia and China the ability to restrict the flow of information to their citizens would seem to call for opponents to be shouting their objections from the rooftops. Instead, there has been no presidential statement or comment from Secretary Clinton, just a blog entry by a minor White House office.

Fortunately, a more robust response to this erosion of Internet freedom came from the House of Representatives, where a bipartisan group of congressmen on the House Energy and Commerce Committee introduced a resolution calling on the Obama administration to oppose efforts to turn the Internet over to UN regulation. The resolution called on the US delegation to the ITU talks to "promote a global Internet free from government control and preserve and advance the successful multi-stakeholder model that governs the Internet today."[28]

The resolution is sponsored by Representative Mary Bono Mack (R-CA) and has the support of Committee Chairman Fred Upton (R-MI), ranking member Henry Waxman (D-CA), Communications and Technology Subcommittee Chairman Greg Walden (R-OR), and ranking subcommittee member Anna Eshoo (D-CA).

Sounding a clarion call, Congresswoman Bono Mack said that "[t]his year, we're facing an historic referendum on the future of the Internet. For nearly a decade, the United Nations quietly has been angling to become the epicenter of Internet governance. A vote for my resolution is a vote to keep the Internet free from government control and to prevent Russia, China, India and other nations from succeeding in giving the UN unprecedented power over Web content and infrastructure." [29]

Bono Mack warns: "If this power grab is successful, I'm concerned that the next 'Arab Spring' will instead become a 'Russian winter,' where free speech is chilled, not encouraged, and the Internet becomes a wasteland of unfilled hopes, dreams and opportunities. We can't let this happen." [30]

The resolution's Democratic cosponsor, Congresswoman Anna Eshoo, added that "this resolution reaffirms our belief and sends a strong message that international control over the Internet will uproot the innovation, openness and transparency enjoyed by nearly 2.3 billion users around the world." [31]

More and more voices are suddenly speaking out against the UN regulation of the Internet. At a congressional hearing in June 2012, FCC Commissioner Robert McDowell asked, "Does anyone here today believe that these countries' [Russia's and China's] proposals would encourage the continued proliferation of an open and freedom-enhancing Internet?" [32]

House Energy and Commerce Committee Chairman Fred Upton (R-MI) said that an "international regulatory intrusion into the Internet would have disastrous results, not only for the US, but for folks around the world." [33]

But statements from American politicians are not going to derail this effort at global censorship. Only the full mobilization of the more than two billion Internet users worldwide will suffice. It is time they learned of the threat to their liberty and battled to defeat it!

KEEP THE INTERNET FREE!

How do we stop this power grab and keep the Internet free? Richard Whitt, public policy director and managing counsel for Google, emphasized the importance of a cyber-roots rebellion against UN control. "I think a key aspect of this [battle] is that this cannot be the US against the world," said Whitt. "If that is the formula, we lose, plain and simple. This has to be something where we engage with everybody around the world. All of the communities of interest who have a stake, whether they know it right now or not, in the future of the Internet, we have to try to find ways to engage them." [34]

Nina Easton, writing on fortune.com, says that "business leaders beyond Silicon Valley would be smart to sit up and take notice [of the UN initiative]—and fast. American opponents are being seriously outpaced by UN plans to tax and regulate that are already grinding forward in advance of a December treaty negotiation in Dubai." [35]

But what happens if a majority of the 193-member ITU votes for a plan that regulates, censors, and controls the Internet? The United States should walk out of the conference in Dubai and refuse to be bound by its strictures. We should work to persuade our European allies to join us.

If the ITU enacts rules on the Internet and the US and the EU refuse to abide by them or recognize them as binding, Internet administrators and the major online companies and servers will be in a bind. They will face a push-pull that may well lead them to compromise our freedoms in order to appease the ITU.

Another bad outcome would be a compromise—in the tradition of the United Nations. Building on the model of the UN Rio Conferences, the so-called middle ground might recognize ITU jurisdiction over the Internet but restrict its power so it does not regulate content or adopt the other nefarious proposals being put forth by Russia and China.

But a compromise of this sort would be a terrible blow to freedom of speech. Conceding that a global body—where autocrats, corrupt regimes, and tyrants have a voting majority—controls the Internet would be the first step in restricting its freedom.

Since the ITU normally does not vote on proposals, preferring instead to negotiate a consensus, Cerf worries that there may be a series of incremental changes that would, together, doom Internet freedom. He cites a proposal by Arab states changing the definition of "telecommunications" to include "processing" or computer functions. FCC commissioner McDowell warns that such a definitional change would "swallow the Internet's functions with only a tiny edit of existing rules."[36]

Indeed, the way the UN works is that such proposals are always, at least partially, adopted. Once a suggestion is raised and ratified by becoming the subject of high-level UN negotiations, a consensus almost always emerges. In this case, it is easy to see how the United States and Europe, heavily outvoted in the ITU, would focus on watering down the Internet regulations while leaving the basic premise—that the ITU can regulate the Net—fundamentally unchallenged.

To counter this consensus approach, we need a massive sense of public outrage (in this election year) demanding that the United States pull out of these negotiations and the Dubai Conference and refuse to recognize the authority of the ITU or its member states or its UN sponsor to even discuss Internet regulation. This is the time for us to stand up and demand an end to this process before it goes any further.

Would the United States cravenly agree to participate in secret negotiations on proposals by Russia and China to restrict global free speech, free press, or freedom of religion? No way. Yet these talks are just as pernicious and destructive of our liberties.

The Internet must see to its own self-preservation! Its users need to spread word of the UN effort virally and arouse a cyber-roots rebellion against the proposed treaty or even the negotiations concerning it. If we want to preserve our freedom to use the Internet as a free exchange of ideas, we have to act and act soon.

Internet users of the world! Speak up!

PART FIVE

TRANSFER OF WEALTH: THE RIO+20 TREATY

Until June 2012, the United States showered the world with foreign aid. We couldn't afford it. It went to the pockets of third world tyrants and dictators. Countries who received our largesse snubbed us at every turn. And some of the money went to our outright enemies.

But at least we had control over how much we gave and who received the money.

In June 2012, Secretary of State Hillary Clinton journeyed to Rio to attend the twentieth anniversary of the original Rio Conference on global sustainability. There, she set a bold new precedent: She committed the United States to giving the United Nations Environment Programme (UNEP)—an incipient global EPA—$2 billion toward an eventual fund of $100 billion, in turn to be given to the nations of the third world, nominally to assist in their adjustment to global climate change.

There's nothing new about the $2 billion commitment. But what is new is that:

a) It implied an American commitment to an even more massive transfer of wealth running to the full $100 billion; and
b) It left it up to a new "Green Climate Fund" headquartered in Switzerland to decide how to spend the money. We would have no control over who received the funds.

The Green Climate fund was formally created at a UN climate conference in Durban, South Africa, in December 2011. It is to be administered by a twenty-four-nation interim board of trustees. Its short-term goal is to amass $100 billion, including $30 billion in "fast start-up" money that has already been pledged by member nations. Hillary's $2 billion was part of that fund.

Hillary's pledge was made at the Rio+20 Conference, where 190 nations gathered on the twentieth anniversary of the 1992 Rio Conference on global sustainability. They committed themselves to the development of a worldwide "green economy in the context of sustainable development and poverty eradication."[1]

Achim Steiner, UN undersecretary-general and UN Environment Programme (UNEP) executive director, proudly reported that at the Rio+20 Conference, "world leaders and governments have today agreed that a transition to a Green Economy—backed by strong social provisions—offers a key pathway towards a sustainable 21st century."[2]

By lumping a "transition to a green economy" and "strong social provisions" in the same statement, Steiner really announces a new global quid pro quo between the developed and less developed world—a historic linkage between payoffs to third world dictatorships and environmental goals. The conference "agreed that such a transition [to a global green economy] could be an important tool when supported by policies that encourage decent employment, social welfare, and the inclusion and maintenance of the Earth's ecosystems from forest to freshwaters."[3]

Third world autocrats no longer need to beg for foreign aid, but instead can demand payoffs as necessary preconditions for their cooperation in protecting the environment. "If you don't pay us off," these nations are in effect saying, "we will chop down rain forests and refuse to cooperate with you in achieving your green goals."

The novelty of this new form of global extortion, enshrined at the Rio Conference, is that it is the first major step in a global scheme to redistribute resources from the first world nations, whose industry and hard work has created them, to world dictators who can stash the money in Swiss bank accounts.

In more civilized language, the Rio Conference noted that its "decision supports nations wishing to forge ahead with a green economy transition while providing developing economies with the opportunity for access to international support in terms of finance and capacity building."[4]

And who will pay the bill for the "decent employment and social welfare" in third world countries? And who will provide developing nations "wishing to forge ahead with a green economy transition . . . the opportunity for access to international support in terms of finance and capacity building?"[5]

We, the taxpayers of developed nations (a category that does not include China or India), will have that privilege. The Rio+20 Conference admitted the "reality that a transition to an inclusive green economy and the realization of a sustainable century needs to also include the footprints of developed nations as well as developing ones as they aim to eradicate poverty and transit towards a sustainable path."[6]

To be sure the money actually flows as directed, "the Summit also gave the go-ahead to a set of Sustainable Development Goals (SDGs) to bring all nations—rich and poor—into cooperative target setting across a range of challenges from water and land up to food waste around the globe."[7]

These Sustainable Development Goals are not about eating your broccoli and remembering the starving millions when your children eat their supper. It is a far larger effort to regulate every aspect of our global economy, consumption patterns, modes of transportation, lifestyles, and economic decisions in the name of achieving the holy grail of "sustainability."

For the greens and globalists, the Rio+20 Conference is the first big step toward global governance, establishing regulations affecting all aspects of our lives, bending every effort toward their environmental priorities.

It was as a down payment on this transfer of wealth that Secretary of State Clinton proudly chipped in the first $2 billion courtesy of the American taxpayer (without asking Congress first) to "mitigate the effects of climate change" in third world countries.[8]

The third world dictatorships are seeking a Global Climate Fund of $100 billion they say is to help them rein in climate change. At the Copenhagen Conference on Global Warming in December 2009, the rich and poor nations of the world agreed to raise $100 billion "in climate aid by 2020, starting with $30 billion by 2012 for 'fast track' financing."[9]

But negotiators from the rich and poor nations have not yet approved the deal. The *New York Times* reports that "from its inception, the fund has been hamstrung by a lack of practical details of where the money should come from, and by competing visions for how it should achieve its aims."[10]

But there are still high hopes for the $100 billion fund. David G. Victor, an energy expert at the University of California, San Diego, says that "for people focused on the lack of progress in the diplomatic talks, the $100 billion was the great hope for bringing countries together and making a deal. For people keen on fixing the world's economic ills, the $100 billion was supposed to help jumpstart a green economy. For people who want to re-allocate the world's wealth, the $100 billion was a new way to move money from North to South."[11]

In October 2011, the negotiating committee of twenty-five delegates from rich countries and fifteen from poor ones completed its draft treaty to set up the $100 billion fund, but the US and Saudi Arabia blocked its approval. In explaining the reason for the American position, the *Times* noted that "the administration of President Barack Obama has come under pressure from prominent Republicans and others to limit financing for UN climate protection initiatives."[12]

Likely the approval of this slush fund for climate aid is one of those areas in which President Obama is waiting for the increased flexibility he expects in his second term, when he will not have to listen to the conservative voices back in Washington.

Negotiations between the rich and poor nations were briefly imperiled in June 2012 when representatives from the developing nations stalked out of the talks "because wealthy countries were refusing to include the transfer of money and technology" in the deal.[13]

The British newspaper the *Guardian* explained the problem: "amid a global economic slowdown and austerity in Europe rich nations are reluctant to put cash on the table." [14]

In a statement of unfathomable arrogance, Brazilian negotiators said this was no excuse. "We cannot be held hostage to the retraction resulting from financial crises in rich countries. We are here to think about the long term and not about crises that may be overcome in one or two years," said Luiz Alberto Figueiredo, undersecretary at the Brazilian foreign ministry.[15]

Figueiredo equates being "held hostage" with not getting his hands on our money!

THE THIRD WORLD CAN'T WAIT TO STEAL THE MONEY

But what good is aid if you can't steal it?

The third world recipients of the generosity of developed nations are insisting that they be "immune from legal challenges and lawsuits not to mention outside inspections, much like the United Nations itself cannot be affected by decisions rendered by a sovereign nation's government or judicial system." [16]

Why are these third world countries so hung up on immunity from investigation, prosecution, and financial controls?

Fox News reports that they want protection from charges of:

• possible conflicts of interest in their duties,

• breaches of confidentiality in their work,

• violations of the due process rights of those affected by their actions,

• making decisions or actions that are beyond the legal mandate of the organization or its subsidiaries.[17]

Already the United Nations Framework Convention on Climate Change (UNFCCC) has come under fire in a study by consultants for the European Commission that criticized it for a "lack of transparency," "inconsistency of decisions," "conflicts of interest," and extensive support for "unsustainable technology for emissions reduction."[18]

Fox News, one of the few media organs to report on the request of immunity, noted that "the move to grant such immunity to an organization engaged in the redistribution of tens of billions of dollars between some of the wealthiest and the poorest nations in the world unavoidably raises questions and concerns."[19]

Who can forget the outright plundering by UN officials—including then secretary-general Kofi Annan's own son—of Oil-for-Food funds in the 1990s. As documented by an investigation by former Federal Reserve chairman Paul Volcker, the theft of funds ran into the hundreds of millions of dollars that were intended for Iraq's poor.

Since no UN official was prosecuted for stealing Oil-for-Food money, many of these same folks are in on the operations of the UNFCCC and are hungering after the vast sums a Global Climate Fund would bring in.

But the $100 billion is never enough!

The third world wants "$1.9 trillion per year . . . for incremental investments in green technologies," according to UN sources. About $800 billion of this sum will be earmarked for third world countries. Fox News reports, "If the UNFCCC has its way, the new Green Climate Fund would not be answerable to the laws of any nation on earth, while it annually redistributed funds equal to roughly half of President Obama's proposed budget for 2012."[20]

Instead of helping poor countries adjust to climate change, most of the money would likely flow instead into the Swiss bank accounts of third world dictators and UN officials. Otherwise, why would they care so passionately about getting immunity?

TOWARD A GLOBAL EPA

Also central to the globalist agenda was the expansion and empowerment of the United Nations Environment Program (UNEP). The Rio+20 Conference expanded UNEP membership from the current fifty-eight nations to include all the world's governments. Its financial resources were augmented. And it was given the mandate "to use international and national laws to advance sustainability, human and environmental rights and the implementation of environmental treaties."[21]

For now, the UNEP has only the power to issue advisory opinions and to suggest regulations to sovereign nations. But more is coming. A report to the UN in advance of the Rio+20 summit declared that "scaled-up and accelerated international cooperation" is required, with new coordination at "the international, sub-regional, and regional levels." Stronger regulation is needed, and "to avoid the proliferation of national regulations and standards, the use of relevant international standards is essential"—an area where the UN can be very helpful, the report indicates.[22]

For those not fluent in UN-speak, "scaled-up and accelerated international cooperation" means empowering the UNEP to bind nations to its will. New coordination at "the international, sub-regional, and regional levels" means making nations listen to its regulations and obey them. The statement that stronger regulation is needed, that "to avoid the proliferation of national regulations and standards, the use of relevant international standards is essential," means that the United Nations Environment Programme should have the right to override national regulations and impose its views by fiat on the nations of the world.[23]

These are the real aspirations of the globalist/socialists for the UNEP. Their ultimate game plan is spelled out in *Only One Earth*, written by Felix Dodds and Michael Strauss, with a forward by the inimitable Maurice Strong.

That volume, published on the eve of the Rio+20 Conference, calls for an International Court for the Environment (ICE). Noting that "there is currently no mechanism for compliance and enforcement in sustainable development, as exists in other areas, such as war crimes or trade," Dodds and Strauss call for the court to "become the principal court dealing with international environmental law." [24]

It would, they explain, "help to clarify existing treaties and other international environmental obligations for states and for all other parties including trans-national corporations. It would do this through dispute resolution, advisory opinions, and the adjudication of contentious issues presently unclear or unresolved." [25]

The Rio+20 globalists also established a ten-year plan to shift governmental procurement—in all nations and at all levels—toward goods and services that enhance their environmental goals. Noting that such purchases account for 15–25 percent of the economies of developed nations and an even larger share in poorer countries, the Rio+20 Conference sought to get all countries to alter their purchasing policies to make them greener.

But the real future thrust of environmental regulation will come against private businesses. The Rio+20 Conference lamented that only "an estimated 25 per cent of the 20,000 companies tracked by Bloomberg are reporting their environmental, social and governance footprints—but 75 per cent are not." [26]

The conference urged all companies to report their environmental and social impacts. That, of course, is the first step. Armed with this disclosure, the global/environmentalists will seek to reward and punish companies based on their environmental and social policies.

Rio called for helping "pension funds to invest in companies with a long-term perspective of profits through sustainability reporting while assisting governments in measuring the contribution of multi-nationals towards national sustainability goals." [27]

In other words, if you pay off the third world, the UNEP will make sure you get contracts, investments, and regulatory support. If not, watch out!

As part of their plan for reshaping our global economy, the Rio+20 Conference called for the replacement of Gross Domestic Product (GDP) as the central measurement of national wealth. Condemning the "narrowness" of GDP as a measurement of economies, it called for a new measurement that would "encourage governments to push forward on requiring companies to report their environmental, social, and governance footprints." [28]

Once private companies measure the extent to which their operations drain the world's wealth through adverse economic or social policies, the UN wants to recalculate the GDP of each country to subtract the negative consequences of its growth.

The vector of this new push is easy to recognize. It would have each company admit and quantify how much it has subtracted from world and national wealth by extracting minerals, endangering the environment, laying off workers, closing plants, etc. By measuring this "environmental and social damage," the UN lays the predicate for fining or taxing or otherwise regulating companies and nations for their damaging policies and programs.

The participants at the Rio+20 were not happy with the outcome despite its evident progress toward global governance. They want mandatory and binding global governance to control all issues related to the global economy, environmental policies, third world development, and the transfer of wealth to poor nations. Anything less is inadequate. But they are patient and keep coming back for more bites at the apple.

The *New York Times* reported sadly that the Rio+20 conference agreed on "so few specifics, so few targets, so few tangible decisions . . . that some participants were derisively calling it 'Rio Minus 20.' " [29]

Kumi Naidoo, executive director of Greenpeace, was particularly dissatisfied, calling the Rio+20 Conference "a failure of epic proportions." [30]

The radical greens all piled on. Lasse Gustavsson, executive director for conservation at the World Wildlife Fund, said that "sophisticated

UN diplomacy has given us nothing more than more poverty, more conflict and more environmental destruction." [31]

The *Times* noted that "the final statement from Rio . . . is 283 paragraphs of kumbaya that 'affirm,' 'recognize,' 'underscore,' 'urge' and 'acknowledge' seemingly every green initiative and environmental problem from water crises and creeping deserts to climate change and overfishing. Women's rights, indigenous peoples, children, mining, tourism, trade unions and the elderly also get shout-outs in the document. The word 'reaffirm' is used 60 times." [32]

The German daily newspaper *Süddeutsche Zeitung* editorialized:

> To be sure, all of the great questions facing humanity make an appearance in the document, but without any attempt at a binding agreement. The Rio+20 conference, which really should have provided a new spark, has instead shined the spotlight on global timidity. Postpone, consider, examine: Even the conference motto—"The Future We Want"—sounds like an insult. If this is the future we want, then good night.
>
> If all countries are satisfied with the lowest common denominator, if they no longer want to discuss what needs to be discussed . . . then the dikes are open. There is no need any more for a conference of 50,000 attendees. Resolutions that are so wishy-washy can be interpreted by every member state as they wish. No one needs Rio. [33]

Doubtless, the greens would have been much happier if, instead of the words "affirm," "recognize," "underscore," "urge," and "acknowledge," the Rio final document included more robust prose like "require," "regulate," "mandatory," and "dictated." But, there's always tomorrow.

But the conference did provide a clear indication of where the environmentalists and globalists are heading. The *Washington Post* reports that "some of the biggest issues activists wanted to see in the document that didn't make it in included a call to end subsidies for fossil fuels, language underscoring the reproductive rights of women, and some words on how nations might mutually agree to protect the high seas, areas that fall outside any national jurisdictions."[34]

The *Post* quotes Greenpeace's Kumi Naidoo as saying: "[W]e saw anything of value in the early text getting removed one by one. What is left is the clear sense that the future we want is not one our leaders can actually deliver. We now need to turn the anger people around the world are feeling into creative, thoughtful and meaningful action."[35]

Rio may not have given the globalists all they wanted, but they received a lot. And we will give them more and more and more unless we realize that their real goal is the forcible transfer of our wealth to them and the surrender of our national sovereignty to a world body.

PART SIX

UN SUPREMACY OVER OUR COURTS

Not content with grabbing global jurisdiction of the oceans and attempting to control the Internet, the globalists at the United Nations are determined to get the United States to knuckle under to the jurisdiction of the International Criminal Court, creating a court superior to our own US Supreme Court.

The International Criminal Court, organized by the United Nations, is battling to gain worldwide acceptance. Already 120 countries have signed on to the court and thirty-two others have signed the treaty recognizing its jurisdiction, but have not yet ratified it.

But until the court can claim jurisdiction over the United States, Russia, and China, it cannot hold sway over the world. None of the big three have signed on.

But President Obama and Secretary Clinton have begun to move in that direction and will likely move further in a second term—should Obama win one—or even in the lame-duck part of this term. (Even if the Senate does not ratify this treaty, under the Vienna Convention—see page 30—we must abide by it until we explicitly renounce it.)

President Bill Clinton did actually sign the treaty in 2000, but he did not submit it to the Senate for ratification because he had problems with some of its provisions. President George W. Bush renounced the treaty and, now, Obama is cozying up to it again.

State Department legal counselor Harold Koh said, "After 12 years, I think we have reset the default on the US relationship with the Court from hostility to positive engagement. In this case, principled engagement worked to protect our interest, to improve the outcome, and to bring us renewed international goodwill."[1]

But that "international goodwill" comes with quite a price!

NO WAR WITHOUT UN APPROVAL

The International Criminal Court is a typical UN bait-and-switch routine. Nominally established to bring dictator/war criminals to justice, its real purpose is to hamstring the US military and force it to abide by UN Security Council rule and regulation. The globalists are using the reasonable desire to get an international court to catch war criminals to restrict the use of military force without the approval of the Security Council—that is to say, without Russian and Chinese approval.

The Treaty of Rome creates a new international crime of "aggression," which means "the use of armed force by one State against another State without the justification of self-defense or authorization by the [UN] Security Council."[2] Under the terms of the court's operation, US presidents who went to war without council approval are liable to arrest, prosecution, and punishment by the International Criminal Court after they leave office.

Former president George W. Bush was planning a trip to Switzerland, where he was to be the keynote speaker at a Jewish charity gala. But Reuters reported that "pressure [was] building on the Swiss government to arrest him . . . if he entered the country," since Switzerland is a signatory to the ICC. On December 2, 2011, Amnesty International called for Bush's arrest while he was touring East Africa. Bush canceled his trip to Switzerland "due to the risk of legal action against him for alleged torture." He went to East Africa without incident.[3]

American negotiators succeeded in getting an amendment to the Rome treaty passed that permitted signatories to opt out of the provisions governing the crime of aggression, but it is worth noting that even though the US is not a signatory to the treaty, Bush was still in jeopardy if he had set foot on Swiss territory.

In any event, the ICC's powers are very elastic. The Rome Treaty says that the court "shall satisfy itself that it has jurisdiction in any case brought before it."[4]

As with many of the UN treaties, the carefully crafted protections and codicils on which our diplomats insist can be swept aside by the body the treaty creates in years ahead without any need to go back to the signatories for approval.

OBAMA'S READY TO SIGN

The evidence that Obama is planning to move toward membership in the ICC is overwhelming. While he has neither signed the treaty yet nor submitted it for Senate ratification, US Ambassador-at-Large for War Crimes Issues Stephen Rapp told the media "our government has now made the decision that Americans will return to engagement at the ICC." The US participated as an observer at the ICC annual meeting in 2010, the first time we sent a delegation to such a meeting.[5]

Secretary of State Hillary Clinton told the Senate Foreign Relations Committee that the US would end its "hostility" to the ICC. Susan Rice, US ambassador to the UN, expressed support for the ICC investigations in the Sudan.

President George W. Bush, on the other hand, was very negative on the ICC and even renounced American cooperation with it, stating that the United States has no legal obligations arising from its signature on the Rome Treaty. He was particularly worried that the ICC might prosecute American soldiers deployed in Iraq, Afghanistan, or other countries and insisted on concluding bilateral agreements with more than one hundred nations hosting our troops, specifying that they would not hand over our personnel to the court for trial.

Now President Obama has removed the sanctions that governed those bilateral agreements, and so has signaled our willingness to cooperate with the court.

$100 MILLION, 700 STAFF, AND ONE INDICTMENT

The ICC does a terrible job of the task for which it was nominally created: the prosecution of human rights violators. In ten years of operation, it has accumulated a staff of seven hundred and spends an annual
budget of $100 million. It has, according to the *Wall Street Journal*, "so
far completed precisely one trial—that of Thomas Lubanga, a com-
mander in the civil war in Congo. It took three years and ended with a
conviction on March 14, 1012. The appeals have not begun. A few other
trials are ongoing or set to begin. Even by the low standards of international tribunals, this performance should raise an eyebrow."[6]

While 120 countries have signed on to the ICC, few of the really bad
actors have done so. The *Journal* reports that the court's membership
"includes few authoritarian countries that employ repression or conduct military operations. Mostly democracies with some semblance of
rule of law have joined."[7] Since the ICC cannot intervene unless a nation is a signatory to the treaty, it doesn't get much business.

But the possible implications of this court are terrifying. It would
have the right, if we signed on, to prosecute Americans for crimes committed on American soil. If a person had already been acquitted by our
own courts, it could indict and try him anew without any restrictions
on double jeopardy.

The court could even overrule decisions of our own Supreme Court
if we become a party to its jurisdiction.

And the ICC has none of our constitutional protections. It has no
trial by jury, no right to a speedy trial, no separation of prosecutorial
and judicial functions (the judge and the prosecutor are the same person). It has no protections against search and seizure and does not follow American jurisprudence.

Some people have cited the court's inability to go after war criminals
as a reason to strengthen its jurisdiction, but Eric Posner, a professor at
the University of Chicago Law School, drew the opposite conclusion,
writing in the *Journal*, "Now . . . it is clear that the ICC will serve no

country's interests, let alone international justice. . . . It is too weak to deter atrocities, end impunity, or keep the peace, but it is strong enough to serve as an irritant in international relations."[8]

But the globalists will continue to press for ICC jurisdiction, always remembering that the court is the judge of its own powers. While their initial sales pitch for the court sounds impressive—the prosecution of war criminals—it really is a heavily disguised attempt to bring the United States and our military under the jurisdiction of a global court. If the Law of the Sea Treaty is a threat to our naval dominance, the ICC is poised to restrict our military power.

We must be vigilant on this issue and move quickly to defeat it should the Obama administration move to resurrect the court and deepen American participation.

PART SEVEN

GLOBALIST CONTROL OF SPACE

Even as the UN tries to take over control of the seas, the globalists are also pushing for international control of outer space. In January 2012, Hillary Clinton announced we would enter into negotiations with the European Union and other "space-faring" nations to develop a Code of Conduct for Outer Space Activities.

On its surface, the code seems to be aimed at keeping outer space tidy by curbing the growing amount of debris in outer space. It is, literally, an anti-littering agreement.

Rose Gottemoeller, acting undersecretary of state for arms control and international security, explains that "orbital debris and irresponsible actions in space have increased the chance of collisions that could have damaging consequences for the United States and others. As more nations and organizations use space, the United States must work with our allies and partners to minimize these problems. The United States is joining with the European Union and others to develop an International Code of Conduct for Outer Space Activities to reduce the potential threat to American space assets by endorsing nonbinding best practices and transparency and confidence-building measures."[1]

A BACKDOOR BAN ON DEFENSIVE SPACE WEAPONS

But Taylor Dinerman, of the Gatestone Institute, explains the code's real purpose: "What this Code would, in fact, ban is what the Europeans, the Russians, and the Chinese see as American 'space weapons.' The code is designed to prevent the United States and other liberal democracies from deploying systems actively to defend their own satellites, while it would allow Russia, China, and just about anyone else to continue their space weapons program, probably with only minimal cosmetic changes."[2]

To curb debris in outer space, the code would prohibit the launch of any missile or satellite that might contribute to litter in outer space. This would ban defensive space-based anti-missile satellites and weapons systems designed to defend against nuclear attack. (The theory is that such systems would contribute to debris by destroying missiles as they fly through space en route to targets in other nations.)

The potential for the development of effective defenses against missile attack has been a hot-button issue ever since the signing of the Anti-Ballistic Missile Treaty (ABM) in 1972. Back in the Cold War, both sides worried overtime about the possibility that the other would develop a "first strike capability," which would allow it to attack first and get away with it. As intercontinental ballistic missiles (ICBMs) became more accurate, arms control advocates worried that they had become a first-strike weapon. So precise was the ability to target these weapons that they could literally travel five thousand miles and actually enter the silos of enemy missiles poised to retaliate, and destroy them before they could be launched.

Compounding this worry was the chance that one side or the other (most likely the US) would develop an effective defense against incoming missiles, which would give it the ability to attack with impunity and without worrying about being wiped out in a retaliatory strike.

These fears led the US and the Soviet Union to sign the Anti-Ballistic Missile (ABM) Treaty in 1972, sharply limiting the development, testing, and deployment of defensive weapons systems.

Reagan danced to the edge of the limits of the ABM Treaty as he developed his Strategic Defense Initiative, dubbed Star Wars by his opponents. Exploiting America's vast lead in computer technology, he sought to develop a shield to protect us from incoming missiles.

The left throughout the world was outraged by Star Wars and, although it was never really developed, fighting against defensive weapons became a cause célèbre on the left.

George W. Bush opted out of the ABM Treaty (the document allowed this) in 2002 and announced that we would not be bound by its provisions any longer. The Bush administration noted that the real threat was no longer a massive Soviet missile strike, but terrorist or rogue states like Iran or North Korea launching missiles to hit the US or Israel. While Star Wars was never able to stop twelve thousand Soviet ICBMs from hitting American targets, it has developed to the point where it can be relied upon to shoot down smaller numbers of missiles.

American plans to base defensive missiles in postcommunist Eastern Europe raised Russian hackles and rallied the European left to oppose the deployment. But, to be truly effective, anti-missile systems need to be based in outer space, where they can hit enemy missiles during their slow-moving launch phase. This strategy has the added advantage that the radioactive debris would fall on the aggressor nation.

Now the European left has devised a backdoor way to stop defense deployments of outer space weapons—the Code of Conduct.

But, as John Bolton points out, we have vital security interests in space that the proposed code may hobble. Bolton writes, "Outer space has become the next frontier for American national security and business. From space, we follow terrorists and intercept their communications, detect foreign military deployments, and monitor a proliferation of unconventional weapons. Our Global Positioning System gives us targeting and tactical advantages, spacecraft create image-rich maps, and satellites beam data around the world."[3]

And, we hope, we can deploy satellites and anti-missile missiles to shoot down whatever Tehran and Pyongyang are prepared to launch against us.

The Europeans have been at work on a Code of Conduct for four years. In January 2012, Hillary announced that the US would not join the EU code as a signatory, but would promise to abide by its provisions even as we proceeded to negotiate an international code of conduct for space. Bolton calls this maneuver "a transparent end run around the constitutional requirement that the Senate ratify all treaties."[4]

Bolton explains that "Obama is eroding American sovereignty on the sly. He knows that an arms-control treaty for space is unlikely. He barely managed to push the new strategic arms reduction treaty with Russia—a bad deal—through the Senate."[5] So, Bolton argues, he and Hillary are cooking up a "code of conduct" to limit US activities without requiring Senate approval.

The administration argues that the code exempts security activities that are for self-defense, but Bolton points out that this "term [is] often defined narrowly to include only cross-border attacks. We should not take the unnecessary risk that our rivals will exploit such ambiguity to prevent legitimate American actions. Taken literally, the European Union code would interfere with our ability to develop antiballistic missile systems in space, test antisatellite weapons and gather intelligence."[6]

ADVANTAGE: CHINA

And, of course, our adversaries won't give the code a second thought. In 2007, China created about half of the outer space debris currently encircling the earth when it shot down a weather satellite. The code would do little to stop Iran, North Korea, Russia, or China from using outer space to counter US technological advantages.

Bolton says that "in a war, China could potentially destroy our satellites and still retain its own GPS capabilities."[7] An analysis prepared by the Joint Chiefs of Staff and submitted to the House Armed Services Committee says that "if the United States were to make a good-faith effort at implementing the requirements of the draft Code, it would most likely have an adverse impact on military operations."[8]

Because it could not hope to get the Code of Conduct through the Senate, the Obama administration maintains that it is not a binding treaty, but only a voluntary guideline for conduct. Michael Listner, of *Space Safety Magazine*, explains that "the administration asserts that since both the European Code of Conduct and the proposed International Code of Conduct are not intended to be legally binding treaties, the administration is not required to seek the advice and consent Congress, nor does it require Congressional intervention while negotiating it."[9]

But, while technically the code is not legally binding, congressmen have been quick to note that it would guide the writing and implementation of regulations that would govern NASA, the Defense Department, and commercial firms operating in space.

Congressmen Michael Turner (R-OH) and Joe Heck (R-NV) and Senators John Kyl (R-AZ) and Jeff Sessions (R-AL) argue that while the code would be nonbinding, it would nonetheless "require the Department of Defense and the intelligence community to implement regulations, which would be binding and could influence both the national and economic security of the United States."[10] The letter also warns that the regulations could impede the "growing commercial space market and the jobs that are created from it."[11]

Dr. Robert Zubrin, president of Pioneer Astronautics and the author of *Energy Victory*, gives a fuller explanation of why the code would be de facto binding on the US:

> Imagine you are a Pentagon colonel, trying to advance your program to develop an anti-satellite weapon system. You need to conduct an in-space test to validate it. You will be told by the brass above you to forget it, because such a test would violate the Code, and it's far above their pay grade to do anything to alter the rules. Now imagine that you are a scientist or engineer doing defense work. You have a new idea for an anti-satellite system, but its development would require in-space testing that might create space debris. Your proposal to start development will be rejected on sight, should you be so intemperate as to not censor the idea yourself.[12]

Zubrin cites as an example of how such a code can become binding in fact, the "planetary protection" agreements reached by the international nongovernmental Committee of Space Research (COSPAR), which have "crippled NASA efforts to mount a mission to Mars to retrieve samples of its soil." He explains that a few bureaucrats meeting together at COSPAR come to an agreement imposing all sorts of difficult requirements on any sample return mission in order to avoid the (nonexistent) threat of back-contamination of Mars. For example, COSPAR requires that the MSR mission "break the chain" of contact between the Mars surface and Earth, which means that instead of directly returning the sample from Mars, there will need to be an autonomous rendezvous and dock in Mars orbit (which has never been done), and the mission will have to be done with two spacecraft, instead of one, increasing costs and greatly adding to mission risk (since BOTH spacecraft need to succeed in order for the mission to succeed). As a result of such imperatives, current NASA designs for the MSR mission are excessively complex and expensive, so much so that the program is now dead in the water. But if you challenge the engineers involved on why they incorporated such irrational features into their design, they will answer that they had to do so, because our COSPAR agreements require it. Thus the mission is killed in the design phase, because it is far above the pay grade of the engineering teams attempting to make it a reality to change the rules. The same dynamic would take hold to block the work of those seeking to develop space defense systems should the Code be put in place.[13]

The fact is that the Obama administration is using the Code of Conduct for Outer Space Activities to shift momentum away from a robust development of space defense, even at a time when it has had little success in curbing the missile programs of Iran and North Korea. Space-based interceptors and satellites are our best protection against these threats and Obama seems intent on giving it away.

But the broader point of the Code of Conduct is that it takes yet another sphere of activity now dominated by the United States and attempts to subject it to global regulation and governance. With the complicity and outright assistance of the Obama administration, we are giving the global community control of the seas and now of space.

PART EIGHT

TAXING THE US WITHOUT OUR APPROVAL

The radical globalists and their environmentalist allies are determined to get their hands on America's wealth any way they can. Recently, the European Union decreed that it would levy a tax—without US approval—on airline flights to and from the United States. The tax—in addition to that permitted by international treaty on all air tickets—would be to compensate for the carbon emitted by airline fuel.

The EU would give this money to give to third world nations to help them deal with climate change.

Officially, the EU demanded that the US and other nations report to Europe on the level of greenhouse gas emissions from their airplanes flying to and from Europe. If the airplanes did not reduce their emissions, the EU would impose a tax on them equal to an estimated $57 on a one-way ticket from New York to London. Collection of the tax is slated to begin in 2013. Once fully enforced, it will cost American air carriers more than $3 billion between now and 2020.

China and India have refused to comply with the reporting requirements and the US and twenty-five other countries are threatening retaliation.

The US attacked the EU tax. " 'The European Union is imposing this on US carriers without our agreement,' Wendell Albright, director of the Office of Aviation Negotiations at the State Department, said. . . . 'It is for the US to decide on targets or appropriate action for US airlines with respect to greenhouse gas emissions.' " [1]

The United States airline industry vigorously challenged the EU's legal right to regulate and tax a US company for conduct that is not connected to the EU and filed suit in the European Court of Justice, the European Union's highest court.

However this dispute is resolved, the essential fact remains: Europe is claiming the power to tax the United States without our consent.

We already, of course, require airlines to collect taxes, but these levies spring from international agreements, not from unilateral actions.

For example, the US currently imposes a tax of $16.70 on all international flights originating or terminating in the United States. But our taxing powers are sharply limited by international treaties.

The EU tax is unilateral, without asking for consent from the US or other nations.

But it is a panacea for the globalists and environmentalists. Here they can tax the United States and distribute the money to the third world as they see fit!

Obviously, the tax will reduce the flow of American tourists, with their much-desired dollars, to Europe. Countries like Italy, France, Spain, and Britain, which heavily depend on American tourist money, will suffer. But to the globalists, the ability to tax America is irresistible.

This tax is being imposed despite the fact that most of a New York–London flight is over international waters, not EU countries. So where does the EU get the jurisdiction to tax American companies for greenhouse gas emissions over the ocean? When questioned, the bureaucrats at the EU don't really provide any legal defense for their unprecedented actions. Instead, they simply claim that someone had to do it. Someone had to save the planet. So they stepped up to the plate—and they're not backing down. But legalities have not stopped the EU bureaucrats from doing whatever it wants to do, including enacting aggressive environmental protection legislation with extraterritorial implications.

The global community, however, has its eye on much broader taxes to reap a bounty for the third world from American efforts and hard work. Nile Gardiner, writing in the *Telegraph*, explains that "a group of United Nations 'independent experts' is pushing the European Union to back a global financial transactions tax to 'offset the costs of the enduring economic, financial, fuel, climate and food crises and to protect basic human rights.'"[2]

The UN continued to press the case for the new tax:

"Where the world financial crisis has brought about the loss of millions of jobs, socialized private debt burdens and now risks causing significant human rights regressions through wide-ranging austerity packages, a financial transaction tax (FTT) is a pragmatic tool for providing the means for governments to protect and fulfill the human rights of their people," said the rights experts on extreme poverty, food, business, foreign debt and international solidarity. EU countries must take bold leadership now to pave the way towards what should eventually be a global FTT.[3]

The UN doesn't hide its goal, income redistribution, noting that "it is high time that governments re-examine the basic redistributive role of taxation to ensure that wealthier individuals and the financial sector contribute their fair share of the tax burden."[4]

The demerits of the global tax aside, the idea that an international entity—the EU, the UN, or the G-20 group of nations—would impose a tax on American citizens and banks is outrageous. Our most fundamental sovereign right is the power of Congress to tax us. Ever since the Magna Carta, the principle has been honored in democracies of "no taxation without representation." To backslide on this rule in order to line the pockets of third world dictators is a very dangerous and bad idea.

PART NINE

AGENDA 21: TELLING US HOW TO LIVE

The single most intrusive—and most ambitious—of the global initiatives that are under way as part of the effort to battle climate change is Agenda 21.

This set of principles, adopted at the First Rio Conference in 1992, spells out how each of us must live in the new world order. We need to leave rural areas, low-density suburbs, and leafy small towns and aggregate in big cities and crowded urban areas. Good-bye, Los Angeles. Hello, midtown Manhattan. Why? So we don't need to drive. We contribute to greenhouse gas emissions when we get behind the wheel. Bikes will become the order of the future.

Like Stalin's collectivization in the 1920s and '30s and the British Enclosure Acts in the nineteenth century, the goal is to force a vast population movement, in this case so we don't emit greenhouse gases.

Agenda 21 began as a long series of recommendations adopted at the First Rio Conference in 1992. Initially, they were really just suggestions to local zoning and planning boards on how to develop more "sustainable" communities. But the movement is gathering to make it the norm for land use decisions at the local level. More and more zoning boards are molding their plans to its contours. Cities are approving or vetoing land use plans based on Agenda 21. It is beginning really to structure how we live.

In *Screwed!*, we set out how Agenda 21 is influencing local communities around the nation.

Its requirements are all in the name of stopping climate change, but, in fact, through voluntary action and citizen education, we are reducing greenhouse gas emissions on our own. Without being herded into high density living arrangements.

- We are driving less. Per capita vehicle mileage is down by 7 percent in the past five years and is continuing to drop.

- One in ten coal-fired energy plants has converted to lower-emission natural gas in the past five years and the trend is accelerating.

- Automobile energy efficiency is continuing to climb steeply.

- Oil use for home heating is down by two-thirds in the past decade.

- Overall, we have reduced our use of oil by 5 percent since 2000 even as our population has grown by 30 million people.

Total US greenhouse gas emissions are down by 10 percent since 2006 and are on schedule to drop by another 10–20 percent by 2020.

We don't need to change the fundamentals of our lives. Greater energy conservation and higher vehicle mileage are the answers. Not a radical change in how we live.

Sorry, environmentalists. We are doing it the American way.

PART TEN

GLOBAL GOVERNANCE: WHO WOULD OUR BEDFELLOWS BE?

The oft-stated goal of global governance—one-world government—begs the question of whether such rule would be democratic and freedom loving or autocratic and arbitrary. Would the world government be fundamentally honest, albeit with a few bad apples, or would it be dominated by kleptocracies—governments whose rulers are only intent on stealing and plundering their way to mega-wealth? Would it be respectful of human rights or ride roughshod over them as happens in many parts of the world?

The fact is that the nations we would be entrusting with our sovereignty are not worthy of the trust. Were this a better world, filled with better nations and rulers, it would be different. But the world is crammed with tiny nations—barely as large as any of our states—who could easily gang up on us and become the tail that wags the dog. And far too many of the nations of the world—more, much more, than would be needed to outvote us—are autocratic, not free, corrupt, and regular violators of human rights.

It is one thing for those of us on the East Coast of the United States to trust our destiny to the voters of the West Coast or the South or the Midwest. It is quite another to give that power to Russia, China, or a collection of tiny, lightly populated, third world autocracies, riddled with corruption and dedicated to the enrichment of their leaders. These are not the kind of bedfellows we want in our government. They are not worthy of entrusting our sovereignty to them.

So let's examine those who would come to rule us in any global governance scheme.

RULE OF THE LILLIPUTIANS: HOW
TINY NATIONS OUTVOTE US

The fundamental concept underscoring global governance is the principle of one nation, one vote. All UN conferences and decision-making bodies—with the sole exception of the Security Council—operate on this principle. With 193 countries in the United Nations, a coalition of very small nations exercises a disproportionate power.

Is the principle of one nation, one vote an appropriate basis for global governance?

It takes 97 nations to constitute a majority of the 193 UN members. But it is possible that a majority of tiny nations could coalesce and outvote the rest. The 97 least-populated UN members have a combined census of only 241 million inhabitants—about one-quarter less than the population of the United States (310 million). These nations, representing only 241 million people, comprise less than 4 percent of the world's 7 billion people, but together they can determine the direction of its decisions.

Many of these countries are really tiny, their nationhood a result of being an island or remote from population centers. Forty countries—enough to outvote the members of NATO—have populations of less than one million people and thirteen have fewer than one hundred thousand people. The most populated of the 97 smaller countries—which, again, can constitute a majority of voting members of the UN—is Bulgaria, with a population of just over 7 million. That's smaller than the population of the five boroughs of New York City!

What kind of global government can be predicated on a system in which Monaco (33,000), San Marino (33,000), Palau (20,000), Tuvalu (20,000), and Nauru (10,000) can outvote China (1.3 billion), India (1.2 billion), and the United States (310 million)?

Permitting these minuscule countries to cast one vote each summons the memory of the old pocket boroughs that were represented by one member each in the British House of Commons for centuries.

Wealthy landowners would get their own estate and the surrounding town—largely populated by their servants—declared a constituency and become entitled to their own personal member of Parliament. Apportionment of seats being what it was, these tiny districts would often outvote the big cities of the UK.

The US Supreme Court realized the injustice of apportioning power based on any measurement other than population when it struck down legislative districts at the state and local level where seats were not allocated based on the number of inhabitants. It was common practice in the state senates of forty-nine states (Nebraska is unicameral) to allocate seats by county, mirroring the composition of the US Senate, where each state gets two members. This distorted legislative apportionment permitted rural counties to outvote the big cities and perpetuate the power of the rural squires who dominated politics in New York, Pennsylvania, Massachusetts, and many eastern states.

The system came to be derided as "one cow, one vote" and met its doom at the hands of the Supreme Court in the reapportionment cases of 1964. The justices ruled that both houses of the state legislatures must be apportioned based only on population. They distinguished state senates from the US Senate because the Constitution explicitly mandates two members from each state for the latter. This provision, of course, stems from the fact that the early United States was a federation of thirteen sovereign states that had won their independence from Great Britain.

It is not merely that it is unfair for St. Kitts and Nevis in the Caribbean and the Marshall Islands in the Pacific to have votes equal to that of the United States. It is that these tiny islands can have no conception of what things are like in larger countries. How can they cast intelligent votes based on their own life experiences living in nation-states that are really no larger than small towns?

And then there is the potential for corruption. Like the pocket boroughs of old Britain, these tiny countries frequently tend to be one-man, quasi-feudal estates. Their UN delegates vote the interests of the one person who controls the island—or the one company. And, in many cases, that vote can be easily bought by offers of foreign aid, investment, or access to the markets of larger nations.

The potential for corruption and injustice implicit in allowing the tail of 241 million people to wag the dog of 7 billion people in the world is too great to let the system continue.

Here's a list of the 97 smallest nations in the UN who constitute a majority of the world body. These tiny nations can outvote the rest of the world and its 7 billion people.[1]

Rank	Country	Population
97	Bulgaria	7,576,751
98	Tajikistan	7,075,000
99	Papua New Guinea	6,888,000
100	Togo	6,780,000
101	Libya	6,546,000
102	Jordan	6,472,000
103	Paraguay	6,460,000
104	Laos	6,436,000
105	El Salvador	6,194,000
106	Sierra Leone	5,836,000
107	Nicaragua	5,822,000
108	Kyrgyzstan	5,550,000
109	Denmark	5,540,241
110	Slovakia	5,426,645
111	Finland	5,366,100
112	Eritrea	5,224,000
113	Turkmenistan	5,177,000
114	Singapore	4,987,600
115	Norway	4,896,700
116	United Arab Emirates	4,707,000
117	Costa Rica	4,640,000
118	Central African Republic	4,506,000
119	Ireland	4,459,300

120	Georgia	4,436,000
121	Croatia	4,435,056
122	New Zealand	4,383,600
123	Lebanon	4,255,000
124	Bosnia and Herzegovina	3,760,000
125	Congo (Rep.)	3,759,000
126	Moldova	3,563,800
127	Liberia	3,476,608
128	Uruguay	3,372,000
129	Mauritania	3,366,000
130	Lithuania	3,329,227
131	Panama	3,322,576
132	Armenia	3,238,000
133	Albania	3,195,000
134	Kuwait	3,051,000
135	Oman	2,905,000
136	Mongolia	2,768,800
137	Jamaica	2,730,000
138	Latvia	2,237,800
139	Namibia	2,212,000
140	Lesotho	2,084,000
141	Slovenia	2,062,700
142	Macedonia	2,048,620
143	Botswana	1,978,000
144	Gambia	1,751,000
145	Qatar	1,696,563
146	Guinea-Bissau	1,647,000
147	Gabon	1,501,000
148	Trinidad and Tobago	1,344,000
149	Estonia	1,340,021
150	Mauritius	1,297,000
151	Swaziland	1,202,000
152	East Timor	1,171,000
153	Djibouti	879,000
154	Fiji	854,000

155	Bahrain	807,000
156	Cyprus	801,851
157	Guyana	761,000
158	Bhutan	708,000
159	Equatorial Guinea	693,000
160	Comoros	691,000
161	Solomon Islands	536,000
162	Suriname	524,000
163	Cape Verde	513,000
164	Luxembourg	502,207
165	Malta	416,333
166	Brunei	407,000
167	Bahamas	346,000
168	Belize	322,100
169	Iceland	317,900
170	Maldives	314,000
171	Barbados	257,000
172	Vanuatu	246,000
173	Samoa	179,000
174	St. Lucia	174,000
175	Sao Tome and Principe	165,000
176	Micronesia	111,000
177	St. Vincent and the Grenadines	109,000
178	Tonga	104,000
179	Grenada	104,000
180	Kiribati	100,000
181	Antigua and Barbuda	89,000
182	Seychelles	85,000
183	Andorra	84,082
184	Dominica	67,000
185	Marshall Islands	63,000
186	St. Kitts and Nevis	38,960
187	Liechtenstein	35,904
188	Monaco	33,000
189	San Marino	32,386

190	Palau	20,000
191	Tuvalu	10,000
192	Nauru	10,000

At its inception, the Charter for the United Nations carefully vested most of the organization's power in a Security Council dominated by its five permanent members: the United States, Britain, France, Russia, and China, each of whom was given a veto power over the actions of the global body. This formulation stemmed from the fact that the UN was originally formed as an association of the Allied powers, who had emerged victorious from the Second World War. The vital role played by each nation was recognized in giving it the veto power.

The power of the Security Council overshadowed the rest of the UN organization during the Cold War since neither Russia nor the United States and our allies was willing to trust its fate to a roll of the dice in the General Assembly, where each nation has a single vote.

When North Korea, with Chinese help, invaded South Korea in 1949, the Soviet veto would have precluded intervention by the Security Council. The United States and our allies passed the "uniting for peace" resolution in the General Assembly, which became the basis for the UN's intervention in Korea to repel communist aggression. Never again would Russia permit the General Assembly to play such a role.

As the decolonialization movement spread throughout Asia and Africa, membership in the United Nations expanded rapidly.

The original UN General Assembly had 51 members when the organization opened its doors in 1945. By 1959 it had grown to 82 members. The next year, 1960, it spurted in size to 99 as former colonies began to join in large numbers. By 1970 it stood at 127. By 1980 it was 154 and by 1990 the membership of the General Assembly was 159.

Then a second spurt in growth happened as the Soviet Russian and Yugoslav confederations broke apart. Membership soared to 189 in 2000. It now stands at 193.

With each new third world addition to the body, the voting power of the West—and Russia—was diluted and the power of the nations of Asia and Africa grew. A sharp anti-American bias became evident as the General Assembly increased in size.

For example, in 2007, on average, only 18 percent of the members of the General Assembly voted with the United States on any given vote (not counting unanimous votes). In 2008, the percentage was up to 26 percent. Then, under Obama, it rose to 42 percent as the administration moved closer to the opinions of the third world countries. (Some would say that it began to share their anti-American bias.) All told, the United States voted no in the General Assembly more often than any other UN member, even in the 2010 session.[2]

Yet it is this very body—the 193 members of the United Nations—and this very voting system—one nation, one vote—that we are about to vest with enormous power. If the globalists and their Obama administration allies have their way, these 193 nations will decide where we can drill for oil offshore, which sea-lanes shall be open for our navigation, how the global Internet is administered, how much we should pay to third world countries to adjust to climate change, what limits to place on our carbon emissions, and dozens of other topics now consigned to our national, state, and local jurisdictions.

In entering into governance by this worldwide body of 193 equal nations, we are dealing into a card game with a stacked deck. We cannot hope to win. We can't even expect fairness.

With the collapse of the Soviet Union and the end of the Cold War's bipolarity, the power of the Security Council within the UN declined. Now its role is primarily limited to UN military intervention and economic sanctions to keep the peace and, supposedly, to fight aggression. But more and more power has flowed to the General Assembly, and the concept of one nation, one vote has become enshrined as the core principle of global governance.

The diminishing power of the major UN nations is evident in the increasing domination of the Group of 77, a coalition of the poorer nations determined to use the UN as a vehicle to channel money from developed nations to their own needs. Although these countries donate only 12 percent of the UN's operating budget, their combined power has become dominant in the General Assembly.

For example, when the US ambassador to the UN under George W. Bush, John Bolton, pushed through a budget cap on UN spending, these seventy-seven nations, who paid about one-eighth of the cost of UN operations, vetoed the proposal. They saw nothing wrong with continued spiraling growth in spending. As long as they weren't paying the bill.

And when it came to limiting investigations of corruption at the UN and defunding the agencies charged with exposing fraud, it was this same group of nations that leveraged the global body. Their brazen efforts to condone and even institutionalize graft and bribery are chronicled in our most recent book, *Screwed!*, in the chapter "The United Nations of Corruption."

Before we dilute our national sovereignty, we are entitled to ask of our fellow nations, with whom we would share power in global governance, are they worthy countries. Are they free? Are they corrupt? Do they respect human rights? The short answer: No, they don't.

ARE THEY FREE?

Freedom House, an organization founded in 1941, at the start of World War II, has kept meticulous and impartial track of the degree of freedom and democracy in each of the world's nations. Every year, it publishes a widely respected report categorizing some nations as free, others as partially free, and still others as not free. Each year, nations move from one category to the other as their political institutions change, revolutions occur, and power changes hands by coups or elections.

Freedom House itself has a storied history. It was founded at the behest of President Franklin D. Roosevelt in the aftermath of his reelection in 1940. Bipartisan, its first cochairs were First Lady Eleanor Roosevelt and the Republican candidate for president FDR had just defeated, Wendell Willkie. Its original purpose was to encourage US intervention in World War II despite isolationist pressure to stay out. Since then, its designation of the degree of freedom in the world's nations has been accepted almost universally (except, of course, by those whose lack of freedom it questions).

In 2011, Freedom House designated 87 of the world's 195 nations (including two non-UN members) as "free." Another 60 countries were "partially free." The other 48 nations were labeled "not free."[3]

Immediately, we see the defect of the one-nation, one-vote rule. The 87 free countries make up a minority of the total UN membership (45 percent).

The 45 percent of the nations that are free have great legitimacy. Their delegates come from democratically elected governments, chosen in free elections. When their delegates speak, they do so with the authority of a government that has been chosen by the consent of the governed.

But who do the delegates from the 55 percent of the world's nations that are only partially free or not free at all represent? Why is it appropriate that they should each have a vote when they stand for nobody but themselves and their own dictatorial or autocratic rulers? Does the delegate from China, for example, speak for his 1.3 billion people or just for the handful that serve on the Communist Party's ruling Politburo? Does Vladimir Putin represent the majority of the Russian people (who chose him in totally rigged, undemocratic elections where the results were intentionally miscounted)?

To lump the free and not-free countries into one world body and to assign each the same voting power mocks the very concept of democracy. The UN is very punctilious about preserving the idea of majority rule and its implication of democratic decision making in the General Assembly. But what kind of democracy is it when 55 percent of the delegates come from governments that do not represent the people who live there?

Even if we base representation on population, we don't do much better in terms of freedom. According to Freedom House, 3 billion people, or 43 percent of the world's population, live in free countries. Two and a half billion—or 35 percent—live in countries that are rated as not free (about half from China with its 1.3 billion people). The rest come from only partly free countries.

Freedom House is rather charitable in its designation "partly free." It defines the category: "A Partly Free country is one in which there is limited respect for political rights and civil liberties. Partly Free states frequently suffer from an environment of corruption, weak rule of law, ethnic and religious strife, and a political landscape in which a single party enjoys dominance despite a certain degree of pluralism."[4]

Freedom House, for example, labels as "partly free" the South American countries under the thumb of Hugo Chavez and his puppets— Venezuela, Ecuador, Bolivia, and Nicaragua. Despite the fact that no elected president has served out his term without being toppled or assassinated, Pakistan is rated as partly free. Liberia, just recovering from the long dictatorship of Charles Taylor, enjoys the partly-free rating as well. The authoritarian, undemocratic regime in Singapore is also rated partly free.

It is no bargain to live in a partly free country.

HERE'S HOW FREEDOM HOUSE RATES THE COUNTRIES OF THE WORLD[5]

Afghanistan	Not Free	Australia	Free
Albania	Partly Free	Austria	Free
Algeria	Not Free	Azerbaijan	Not Free
Andorra	Free	Bahamas	Free
Angola	Not Free	Bahrain	Not Free
Antigua and Barbuda	Free	Bangladesh	Partly Free
Argentina	Free	Barbados	Free
Armenia	Partly Free	Belarus	Not Free

Belgium	Free	Czech Republic	Free
Belize	Free	Denmark	Free
Benin	Free	Djibouti	Not Free
Bhutan	Partly Free	Dominica	Free
Bolivia	Partly Free	Dominican Republic	Free
Bosnia and Herzegovina	Partly Free	East Timor	Partly Free
Botswana	Free	Ecuador	Partly Free
Brazil	Free	Egypt	Not Free
Brunei	Not Free	El Salvador	Free
Bulgaria	Free	Equatorial Guinea	Not Free
Burkina Faso	Partly Free	Eritrea	Not Free
Burma	Not Free	Estonia	Free
Burundi	Partly Free	Ethiopia	Not Free
Cambodia	Not Free	Fiji	Partly Free
Cameroon	Not Free	Finland	Free
Canada	Free	France	Free
Cape Verde	Free	Gabon	Not Free
Central African Republic	Partly Free	Gambia	Not Free
Chad	Not Free	Georgia	Partly Free
Chile	Free	Germany	Free
China	Not Free	Ghana	Free
Colombia	Partly Free	Greece	Free
Comoros	Partly Free	Grenada	Free
Congo (cap. Brazzaville)	Not Free	Guatemala	Partly Free
Congo (cap. Kinshasa)	Not Free	Guinea	Partly Free
Costa Rica	Free	Guinea-Bissau	Partly Free
Côte d'Ivoire	Not Free	Guyana	Free
Croatia	Free	Haiti	Partly Free
Cuba	Not Free	Honduras	Partly Free
Cyprus	Free	Hungary	Free

Iceland	Free	Maldives	Partly Free
India	Free	Mali	Free
Indonesia	Free	Malta	Free
Iran	Not Free	Marshall Islands	Free
Iraq	Not Free	Mauritania	Not Free
Ireland	Free	Mauritius	Free
Israel	Free	Mexico	Partly Free
Italy	Free	Micronesia	Free
Jamaica	Free	Moldova	Partly Free
Japan	Free	Monaco	Free
Jordan	Not Free	Mongolia	Free
Kazakhstan	Not Free	Montenegro	Free
Kenya	Partly Free	Morocco	Partly Free
Kiribati	Free	Mozambique	Partly Free
Kosovo	Partly Free	Namibia	Free
Kuwait	Partly Free	Nauru	Free
Kyrgyzstan	Partly Free	Nepal	Partly Free
Laos	Not Free	Netherlands	Free
Latvia	Free	New Zealand	Free
Lebanon	Partly Free	Nicaragua	Partly Free
Lesotho	Partly Free	Niger	Partly Free
Liberia	Partly Free	Nigeria	Partly Free
Libya	Not Free	North Korea	Not Free
Liechtenstein	Free	Norway	Free
Lithuania	Free	Oman	Not Free
Luxembourg	Free	Pakistan	Partly Free
Macedonia	Partly Free	Palau	Free
Madagascar	Partly Free	Panama	Free
Malawi	Partly Free	Papua New Guinea	Partly Free
Malaysia	Partly Free	Paraguay	Partly Free

Peru	Free	Sudan	Not Free
Philippines	Partly Free	Suriname	Free
Poland	Free	Swaziland	Not Free
Portugal	Free	Sweden	Free
Qatar	Not Free	Switzerland	Free
Romania	Free	Syria	Not Free
Russia	Not Free	Taiwan	Free
Rwanda	Not Free	Tajikistan	Partly Free
St. Kitts and Nevis	Free	Thailand	Partly Free
Saint Lucia	Free	Togo	Partly Free
Saint Vincent and Grenadines	Free	Tonga	Partly Free
Samoa	Free	Trinidad and Tobago	Free
San Marino	Free	Tunisia	Partly Free
São Tomé and Príncipe	Free	Turkey	Partly Free
Saudi Arabia	Not Free	Turkmenistan	Not Free
Senegal	Partly Free	Tuvalu	Free
Serbia	Free	Uganda	Partly Free
Seychelles	Partly Free	Ukraine	Partly Free
Sierra Leone	Partly Free	United Arab Emirates	Not Free
Singapore	Partly Free	United Kingdom	Free
Slovakia	Free	United States	Free
Slovenia	Free	Uruguay	Free
Solomon Islands	Partly Free	Uzbekistan	Not Free
Somalia	Not Free	Vanuatu	Free
South Africa	Free	Venezuela	Partly Free
South Korea	Free	Vietnam	Not Free
South Sudan	Not Free	Yemen	Not Free
Spain	Free	Zambia	Partly Free
Sri Lanka	Partly Free	Zimbabwe	Not Free

So who are we about to surrender our sovereignty to? A world body dominated by small nations, barely the size of one of our states, in which we have only one of 193 votes, where the majority of the countries are not free to choose delegates who represent their own people?

There is nothing inherent in the idea of global governance that is wrong. Indeed, we are all human and we all inhabit the same planet so eventually some form of global government may be appropriate. But today, such a government could only be as strong and just as its component parts. The failure of freedom to spread to more than a minority of the world makes the submersion of our sovereignty into such a worldwide body an act that will lead to the surrender of our freedoms.

The very premise of the United Nations is based on the idea that you take the countries as you find them. Whether they are dictatorships, monarchies, or tyrannies of any description does not matter. As long as they are in de facto control of their populations and landmasses, they are nations entitled to representation and recognition. If the people want to change the government, that's their business. If they want greater freedom, good luck to them. But, in the meantime, the UN takes all comers and does not have a litmus test for freedom.

The United Nations was set up to be a kind of permanent international conference, akin to the gatherings of the top world leaders that formulated policy for the Allies during World War II. Where Stalin, Churchill, and Roosevelt met at Yalta to design the postwar world, now their delegates meet at the United Nations to keep it going and to avert a catastrophic world conflict. That's, of course, why the Security Council—which mimics their wartime conferences—had most of the power in the early days of the United Nations.

But as power shifted to the General Assembly, where each nation cast a vote and none had a veto, the UN's refusal to distinguish between legitimate, democratic governments and autocratic ones becomes harder to justify. And when they meet not to negotiate, but to govern, they are not entitled to the same level of participation.

A value-free acceptance of all comers makes perfect sense in a negotiation where countries meet to discuss mutual problems or resolve conflicts. In those cases, the dictator who runs one country must sit down with the elected leader who rules the other nation on terms of parity and equality. What matters is control, not legitimacy.

If Saudi Arabia is controlled by a king, Russia by a dictator, China by a one-party system, that is none of our business in international negotiations. We have to take them as they are and negotiate to maintain harmony, trade, and peace.

But when the talk switches from horse-trading and negotiation to governance, the idea of including not free governments and according them a vote equal to that cast by free nations is not a wise idea. And to immerse ourselves in a global governing body where a majority of the votes are cast by peoples who are, to some degree or the other, enslaved, makes no sense at all. We must not subject ourselves to the rule of a world body dominated by autocrats.

Nor need we be Gulliver, the 310 million person democracy, being tied down by 97 Lilliputian nations each with populations of 7 million or less, together casting a majority of the votes and bending global policies to their own needs and outlooks.

We are, at least, entitled to a veto—as we have in the Security Council—and should make common government only with fellow democracies committed to human freedom and the consent of the governed.

In a world of nations a majority of whom are not free, there can be no government by consent of the governed and the United States of America should not be part of it.

ARE THEY HONEST?

But our likely new rulers in the third world are not only undemocratic and not free, they are also hopelessly corrupt. A new word had to be created to articulate the degree of corruption: *kleptocracy* (a government based on stealing and graft). These governments are to be distinguished from those in which scandal occasionally or even frequently rears its head. Every government has a few greedy public servants who help themselves to riches and wealth. But they are usually investigated and often punished. But kleptocracies are different. These are governments whose mission is to steal, whose reason for being is to make money for its leaders.

These states are more like criminal gangs than regular governments. Their ruling elites get to serve as presidents, prime ministers, ambassadors, negotiators, delegates, foreign secretaries, and cabinet secretaries. In each position, they are empowered to steal all they can and to share their loot with one another.

To such nations, membership in the United Nations affords entrée to a realm of vast resources there just for the taking. And take they do.

What proportion of the UN membership are kleptocracies?

Once again, we can turn to a reputable international civic group for the answer. Just as Freedom House compiles rankings of countries based on the degree of freedom their people enjoy, so Transparency International rates them based on their propensity toward corruption.

Transparency International defines corruption:

Corruption is the abuse of entrusted power for private gain. [The index] focuses on corruption in the public sector, or corruption which involves public officials, civil servants or politicians. The data sources used to compile the index include questions relating to the abuse of public power and focus on: bribery of public officials, kickbacks in public procurement, embezzlement of public funds, and on questions that probe the strength and effectiveness of anti-corruption efforts in the public sector.[6]

Their methodology is impressive.

- They take a survey of more than seventy thousand households in ninety countries to measure "perceptions and experiences of corruption."[7]

- They interview business executives who export goods and services to learn "the perceived likelihood of their firms [having to] bribe" officials in each nation to whom they sell.[8]

- They issue a Global Corruption Report, which explores corruption in particular sectors or spheres of government operations.[9]

- Finally, they conduct a "series of in-country studies providing an extensive assessment of the strengths and weaknesses of the key institutions that enable good governance and integrity in a country (the executive, legislature, judicial, and anti-corruption agencies among others)."[10]

Based on this extensive research, Transparency International rates every nation on a scale of 1 to 10, with 1 meaning that it is highly corrupt and 10 meaning that it has quite high standards of honesty and integrity.

The results are dismal. Corruption is the order of the day in most countries of the world—the very nations that would rule any global government to which we assent!

About three-quarters of the countries of the world—132 of the 182 nations rated—received less than a 5 (on a 1–10 scale), indicating that they were badly corrupted. Ninety-two (half the countries) got a rating of 3 or less, indicating that corruption had penetrated to its very core. Only fifty of the 182 nations got better than a 5 on the corruption scale!

Here are the rankings for each country:[11]

HONEST NATIONS (rank and score)

1. New Zealand	9.5	4. Sweden	9.3
2. Denmark	9.4	5. Singapore	9.2
2. Finland	9.4	6. Norway	9.0

7. Netherlands	8.9	29. Estonia	6.4
8. Australia	8.8	30. Cyprus	6.3
8. Switzerland	8.8	31. Spain	6.2
10. Canada	8.7	32. Botswana	6.1
11. Luxembourg	8.5	32. Portugal	6.1
12. Hong Kong	8.4	32. Taiwan	6.1
13. Iceland	8.3	35. Slovenia	5.9
14. Germany	8.0	36. Israel	5.8
14. Japan	8.0	36. Saint Vincent and	
16. Austria	7.8	Grenadines	5.8
16. Barbados	7.8	37. Bhutan	5.7
16. United Kingdom	7.8	38. Malta	5.6
19. Belgium	7.5	38. Puerto Rico	5.6
19. Ireland	7.5	40. Cape Verde	5.5
21. Bahamas	7.3	40. Poland	5.5
22. Chile	7.2	42. South Korea	5.4
22. Qatar	7.2	43. Brunei	5.2
24. United States	7.1	43. Dominican Republic	5.2
25. France	7.0	45. Bahrain	5.1
25. St. Lucas	7.0	45. Macau	5.1
25. Uruguay	7.0	45. Mauritius	5.1
28. United Arab Emirates	6.8	49. Rwanda	5.0

CORRUPT NATIONS

50. Costa Rica	4.8	54. Kuwait	4.6
50. Lithuania	4.8	56. Jordan	4.5
50. Oman	4.8	57. Czech Republic	4.4
50. Seychelles	4.8	57. Namibia	4.4
54. Hungary	4.6	57. Saudi Arabia	4.4

60. Malaysia	4.3	80. Colombia	3.4
61. Cuba	4.2	80. El Salvador	3.4
61. Latvia	4.2	80. Greece	3.4
61. Turkey	4.2	80. Morocco	3.4
61. Georgia	4.1	80. Peru	3.4
64. South Africa	4.1	80. Thailand	3.4
66. Croatia	4.0	86. Bulgaria	3.3
66. Montenegro	4.0	86. Jamaica	3.3
66. Slovakia	4.0	86. Panama	3.3
69. Ghana	3.9	86. Serbia	3.3
69. Italy	3.9	86. Sri Lanka	3.3
69. Macedonia	3.9	91. Bosnia and Herzegovina	3.2
69. Samoa	3.9	91. Liberia	3.2
73. Brazil	3.8	91. Trinidad and Tobago	3.2
73. Tunisia	3.8	91. Zambia	3.2
75. China	3.6	95. Albania	3.1
75. Romania	3.6	95. India	3.1
77. Gambia	3.5	95. Kiribati	3.1
77. Lesotho	3.5	95. Swaziland	3.1
77. Vanuatu	3.5	95. Tonga	3.1

VERY CORRUPT NATIONS

100. Argentina	3.0	100. Malawi	3.0
100. Benin	3.0	100. São Tomé and Príncipe	3.0
100. Burkina Faso	3.0	100. Suriname	3.0
100. Djibouti	3.0	100. Tanzania	3.0
100. Gabon	3.0	112. Algeria	2.9
100. Indonesia	3.0	112. Egypt	2.9
100. Madagascar	3.0	112. Kosovo	2.9

112.	Moldova	2.9		143.	Comoros	2.4
112.	Senegal	2.9		143.	Mauritania	2.4
112.	Vietnam	2.9		143.	Nigeria	2.4
118.	Bolivia	2.8		143.	Russia	2.4
118.	Mali	2.8		143.	Timor-Lesta	2.4
120.	Bangladesh	2.7		143.	Togo	2.4
120.	Ecuador	2.7		143.	Uganda	2.4
120.	Ethiopia	2.7		152.	Tajikistan	2.3
120.	Guatemala	2.7		152.	Ukraine	2.3
120.	Iran	2.7		154.	Central African Republic	2.2
120.	Kazakhstan	2.7		154.	Congo Republic	2.2
120.	Mongolia	2.7		154.	Ivory Coast	2.2
120.	Mozambique	2.7		154.	Guinea-Bissau	2.2
120.	Solomon Islands	2.7		154.	Kenya	2.2
129.	Armenia	2.6		154.	Laos	2.2
129.	Dominican Republic	2.6		154.	Nepal	2.2
129.	Honduras	2.6		154.	Papua New Guinea	2.2
129.	Philippines	2.6		154.	Paraguay	2.2
129.	Syria	2.6		164.	Cambodia	2.1
134.	Cameroon	2.5		164.	Guinea	2.1
134.	Eritrea	2.5		164.	Kyrgyzstan	2.1
134.	Guyana	2.5		164.	Yemen	2.1
134.	Lebanon	2.5		168.	Angola	2.0
134.	Maldives	2.5		168.	Chad	2.0
134.	Nicaragua	2.5		168.	Democratic Republic of Congo	2.0
134.	Niger	2.5		168.	Libya	2.0
134.	Pakistan	2.5		172.	Burundi	1.9
134.	Sierra Leone	2.5		172.	Equatorial Guinea	1.9
143.	Azerbaijan	2.4		172.	Venezuela	1.9
143.	Belarus	2.4				

175. Haiti	1.8		180. Afghanistan	1.5
175. Iraq	1.8		182. Myanmar	1.5
177. Sudan	1.6		182. North Korea	1.0
177. Turkmenistan	1.6		182. Somalia	1.0
177. Uzbekistan	1.6			

Are these the nations to whom we are thinking of surrendering our sovereignty, giving them a one-nation, one-vote right to govern us and control our economies, the sea, the Internet, our industries, and many other key aspects of our lives?

But it is not just the member states of the UN that are hopelessly mired in corruption; it is the United Nations itself.

This institutional tolerance of corruption was much in evidence in the 1990s as the UN administered the Oil-for-Food program in Iraq. Established under UN auspices to channel revenues from Iraq's carefully regulated sale of oil to provide food and medicine for its people, starving under the impact of international sanctions, the program became a poster child for corruption. The money mainly went into the pocket of the dictator, Saddam Hussein, and into those of the UN officials charged with administering the program.

The UN corruption demonstrated by the Oil-for-Food program is sickening. But worse—far worse—is the immunity and impunity of those who committed the larceny. They have not been punished or disciplined or even fired. They remain at their desks in the UN headquarters, anxious to see greater globalism enlarge their opportunities for personal enrichment and theft.

The oil-for-food program began in 1990 when the UN imposed economic sanctions against Saddam Hussein. To overturn the sanctions, Saddam worked to loosen the sanctions by pleading that they were starving his people and denying medical care to his children. So the UN decided to allow Saddam to sell limited amounts of oil to feed his people. As a result of his overt efforts to stir up sympathy for his starving people and his covert bribery of top UN officials, Saddam gradually expanded the amount of oil he could sell until the limits were ended entirely.

But the slush fund his oil profits generated found its way into the pockets of a plethora of international politicians often at the highest levels. The program included a 2.2 percent commission on each barrel of oil sold. Over the life of the oil-for-food program, the UN collected $1.9 billion in commissions on the sale of oil.[12]

The program was overseen by the Security Council of the UN, but subsequent investigations revealed that the leaders and UN delegates of three of the five permanent members—Russia, China, and France— were on the take, pocketing commissions as they rolled in.

- France received $4.4 billion in oil contracts.

- Russia received $19 billion in oil deals.

- Kojo Annan, the son of Kofi Annan (then UN secretary-general), received a $10 million contract.

- Alexander Yakovlev of Russia, senior UN procurement officer, pocketed $1 million.

- Benon Sevan, administrator of the oil-for-food program, received $150,000 in cash.

- France's former UN ambassador Jean-Bernard Mérimée received $165,725 in oil allocations from Iraq.

- Rev. Jean-Marie Benjamin, assistant to the Vatican secretary of state, received oil allocations under the program.

- Charles Pasqua, former French interior minister and intimate friend of former French president Jacques Chirac, received oil allocations.

- The Communist Party in Russia, the Russian Orthodox Church, and several Russian oil companies all received oil allocations.

In all, 270 separate people received oil vouchers permitting them to buy Iraqi oil at a discount and then sell it at the higher market price, pocketing the difference.

Former Federal Reserve chairman Paul Volcker, who investigated the program at the behest of the UN, said, "Corruption of the [oil-for-food] program by Saddam and many participants could not have been nearly so pervasive with more disciplined management by the United Nations."[13]

Forty countries and 2,250 companies paid bribes to Saddam under oil-for-food to receive favorable treatment.

No UN official has been criminally prosecuted for bribes or any other crime stemming from the oil-for-food program.

This is the record of corruption at the United Nations. Who can doubt that if the Law of the Sea Treaty is ratified, the billions in oil royalties that flow through the UN will not open the door to the same kind of systematic and universal graft that characterized the oil-for-food program?

New opportunities for corruption-without-consequence are emerging from the initiatives for global governance. If the UN is to administer a vast fund to redistribute wealth to the third world, tax oil royalties from offshore drilling, regulate the Internet, and tax financial transactions and the like, the kleptocracies that make up much of the UN membership can only lick their chops in anticipation.

But won't the UN enforce rules against corruption as it acquires more power? History indicates that it will do nothing at all to clean up its act.

Indeed, the tendency toward corruption—and the blind eye the UN leadership turned to it—that was evident in the 1990s only accelerated with the start of the new millennium.

In 2005, a huge scandal ripped the UN Procurement Department, which was responsible for all purchases made by the organization. Alexander Yakovlev, the head of the department, pled guilty to federal charges of wire fraud, racketeering, and money laundering. Working with his fellow Russian Vladimir Kuznetsov, the head of the UN Budget Oversight Committee, he tipped off bidders for contracts with inside information in return for bribes. Paul Volcker estimated that the Russians made off with $950,000 in bribes and helped contractors win more than $79 million in UN contracts.[14]

A year later, the FBI broke up a drug ring operating right out of the UN mailroom that had smuggled 25 tons of illegal drugs into the United States in 2005–2006.[15]

But what is exceptional about the Yakovlev case and the FBI investigation are not the crimes the UN officials committed, but the fact that they were punished. The case against Yakovlev was brought by the US attorney for the area in which the UN is physically located. The UN not only has never prosecuted one of its own for stealing or anything else, it totally lacks the ability even to try to do so. Such prosecutions of UN officials as the US attorney can bring are the only means of holding UN personnel legally accountable. But these cases are rare because the UN organization systematically hides evidence and permits its delegates to conceal their larceny behind diplomatic immunity.

Volcker complained about what he called "the culture of inaction" that surrounds the UN's efforts at reform. Indeed, the anti-corruption agency at the international body, the Office of Internal Oversight Services (OSIS), can only investigate UN agencies with their permission. Its funding for these inquiries must come from the budgets of the agencies it investigates. David M. Walker, comptroller-general of the United States, said that "UN funding arrangements constrain OIOS's ability to operate independently. . . . OIOS depends on the resources of the funds, programs, and other entities it audits. The managers of these programs can deny OIOS permission to perform work or not pay OIOS for services."[16]

Outrage at UN corruption—and the permissive attitude of the secretary-generals toward it—has led to several attempts in recent years at cleaning up the mess. But each has been thwarted, often by the delegates to the General Assembly from third world nations that don't want their personal candy store to close.

UN Secretary-General Ban Ki-moon hired former US attorney Robert Appleton to investigate corruption in the United Nations. Appleton did a very good job, uncovering massive bribery, larceny, bid-rigging, money laundering, and the like all over the world body. He was rewarded for his services by the General Assembly, which defunded his unit, fired him, and blackballed his staff from ever working for the UN again.

All his findings were swept under the UN rug. Appleton said, "As far as I am aware, significant follow-up [to my investigations] was only made in one case, and that was after significant pressure—including from . . . Congress."[17]

Appleton told Congress that "the most disappointing aspect of my experience in the [UN] organization was not with what we found, but the way in which investigations were received, handled, and addressed by the UN administration and the way in which investigations were politicized by certain member states."[18]

Another anti-corruption agency, the UN Joint Inspection Unit (JIU), was similarly crushed after it also exposed corruption, particularly in the notorious Procurement Department. The General Assembly's Senior Review Group fired the director of the JIU and replaced him and his staff with more compliant and less thorough investigators.[19]

It's not healthy to investigate UN corruption. On December 11, 2011, Secretary-General Ban Ki-moon crippled the UN Dispute Tribunal, a judicial body he himself had established two years before. He stripped its judges of the capacity to protect whistle-blowers. The judges—recruited from outside the UN bureaucracy—charged that the secretary-general who had appointed them was trying to "undermine the integrity and independence" of their court.

Ban Ki-moon stripped the tribunal of its ability to order its decisions to be enforced while they were under appeal to the United Nations Appeals Tribunal. Key was its ability to protect those who had come forward with information from dismissal or demotion. The secretary-general also took away the court's subpoena power and denied it the right to demand that he "produce a document or witness in response to charges of unjust treatment." [20]

This is the same secretary-general who will be given the power to appoint judges to the Law of the Sea Tribunal to adjudicate disputes between the US and other nations should we ratify the LOST.

How can we ever trust him with the power to name the arbiters of the law of the sea and of the resources that lie beneath the waves?

DO THEY RESPECT HUMAN RIGHTS?

Human rights are regularly abused by a great many of the countries with whom we would share our sovereignty if the globalists in the UN have their way. And things are getting worse.

Freedom House notes that

despite a net 37-year gain in support for the values of democracy, multiparty elections, the rule of law, freedom of association, freedom of speech, the rights of minorities and other fundamental, universally valid human rights, the last four years have seen a global decline in freedom. The declines represent the longest period of erosion in political rights and civil liberties in the nearly 40-year history of Freedom in the World. New threats, including heightened attacks on human rights defenders, increased limits on press freedom and attacks on journalists, and significant restrictions on freedom of association have been seen in nearly every corner of the globe. [21]

To understand the values and ideals of our fellow nations and their rulers, we need to understand the depravity with which many of them treat human beings and their sacred rights. We must understand, as we peruse their terrible records, that each of these nations—criminal gangs really—will have the same vote on UN global councils as we do.

Freedom House published a sad list titled "The Worst of the Worst." Unfortunately, their list of the most egregious human rights violators includes China, which sits not only in the General Assembly, but also as a permanent member on the Security Council, where it has a veto over all measures.

Here's the highlights of the Freedom House report of the worst of the worst on human rights in the world:

Belarus

A former member of the Soviet Union, Belarus is still as tightly controlled today by its dictator Alyaksandr Lukashenka as it once was by Stalin. Freedom House reports, "His government . . . uses police violence and other forms of harassment against the political opposition, and blocked independent media from covering demonstrations through systematic intimidation. After releasing all of its political prisoners in 2008, the regime incarcerated more activists in 2009." [22]

"President Lukashenka systematically curtails press freedom," Freedom House reports. "Libel is both a civil and criminal offense, and an August 2008 media law gives the state a monopoly over information about political, social, and economic affairs. The law gives the cabinet control over Internet media. State media are subordinated to the president, and harassment and censorship of independent media are routine." [23]

How comforting that President Lukashenka's handpicked delegates will have a vote equal to ours on issues of Internet freedom if the new telecommunications regulations are confirmed in December in Dubai!

Pity this poor country. After experiencing Stalin's abuses before

World War II, Hitler during it, and repressive communism after it, Belarus is still ruled by a corrupt, absolute dictator. It can't catch a break!

Burma (Myanmar)

Rated as the single most oppressive regime in the world, Burma's military regime governs by arresting and imprisoning political dissidents.

"The State Peace and Development Council (SPDC) rules by decree," Freedom House reports. "It controls all executive, legislative, and judicial powers, suppresses nearly all basic rights, and commits human rights abuses with impunity. Given the lack of transparency and accountability, corruption and economic mismanagement are rampant at both the national and local levels."[24]

"The junta drastically restricts press freedom and owns or controls all newspapers and broadcast media. The authorities practice surveillance at Internet cafes and regularly jails bloggers. Teachers are subject to restrictions on freedom of expression and are held accountable for the political activities of their students. Some of the worst human rights abuses take place in areas populated by ethnic minorities. In these border regions the military arbitrarily detains, beats, rapes, and kills civilians."[25]

Chad

Freedom House reports that this country located right below the Sahara Desert "has never experienced a free and fair transfer of power through elections. Freedom of expression is severely restricted. . . . In 2008, the government imposed a new press law that increased the maximum penalty for false news and defamation to three years in prison, and the maximum penalty for insulting the president to five years. Human rights groups credibly accuse the security forces and rebel groups of killing and torturing with impunity."[26] Charming. And the recent discovery of oil will provide even more excuses for murder.

China (People's Republic of China)

This nation, which sits on the UN Security Council, is the world's most populous and second richest. But Freedom House reminds us of the disreputable foundations on which its government precariously rests. "The Chinese government, aiming to suppress citizen activism and protests during politically sensitive anniversaries . . . resorted to lockdowns on major cities, new restrictions on the Internet, and a renewed campaign against democracy activists, human rights lawyers, and religious minorities. The Chinese Communist Party (CCP) possesses a monopoly on political power; its nine-member Politburo Standing Committee makes most key political decisions and sets government policy. Opposition groups are suppressed, and activists publicly calling for reform of the one-party political system risk arrest and imprisonment. Tens of thousands are thought to be held in prisons and extrajudicial forms of detention for their political or religious views. Despite thousands of prosecutions launched each year and new regulations on open government, corruption remains endemic, particularly at the local level." [27]

"Freedom of the press remains extremely restricted, particularly on topics deemed sensitive by the CCP. During the year, the authorities sought to tighten control over journalists and Internet portals, while employing more sophisticated techniques to manipulate the content circulated via these media. Journalists who do not adhere to party dictates are harassed, fired or jailed." [28]

Given China's efforts to enhance global regulation of the Internet through the United Nations, it is important that while China "is home to the largest number of Internet users globally, the government maintains an elaborate apparatus for censoring and monitoring Internet use, including personal communications, frequently blocking websites it deems politically threatening." [29]

In addition, Freedom House notes that "torture remains widespread, with coerced confessions routinely admitted as evidence. Serious violations of women's rights continue, including domestic violence, human trafficking, and the use of coercive methods to enforce the one-child policy."[30]

Robert Zubrin, the author of the new book *Merchants of Despair*, tells us that between 2000 and 2004, there were 1.25 boys born alive in China to every 1 girl. He concludes, grimly, that this indicates that "one-fifth of all baby girls in China were either being aborted or murdered. In some provinces, the fraction [of girls] eliminated was as high as one-half."[31]

Cuba

Cuba remains stuck in the backwash of its 1957 communist revolution. Freedom House: "Longtime president Fidel Castro and his brother, current president Raul Castro, dominate the one-party political system. The Communist Party of Cuba (PCC) controls all government entities from the national to the local level. All political organization outside the PCC is illegal. Political dissent, whether spoken or written, is a punishable offense, and dissidents frequently receive years of imprisonment for seemingly minor infractions." In 2009, there were more than two hundred political prisoners in Cuban jails.

"Freedom of the press is sharply curtailed, and the media are controlled by the state and the PCC. Independent journalists are subjected to ongoing repression, including terms of hard labor and assaults by state security agents. Access to the Internet remains tightly restricted, and it is difficult for most Cubans to connect in their homes."[32]

Equatorial Guinea

President Teodoro Obiang Nguema Mbasogo is the longest-serving ruler in sub-Saharan Africa. He has been the dictator of this impoverished but oil-rich country for thirty years. CBS News reports that he has been accused "of cannibalism, specifically eating parts of his opponents to gain power."[33] He stays in power by rigging the elections. Freedom

House reports that Equatorial Guinea, a country of just seven hundred thousand people, "has never held credible elections [and] is considered one of the most corrupt countries in the world. . . . Obiang and members of his inner circle continue to amass huge personal profits from the country's oil windfall. The state holds a near-monopoly on broadcast media, and the only Internet service provider is state affiliated, with the government reportedly monitoring Internet communications. The authorities have been accused of widespread human rights abuses, including torture, detention of political opponents, and extrajudicial killings."[34]

Eritrea

On Africa's eastern horn, Eritrea has a form of conscription that binds people to work for the state for much of their lives. Recently, Freedom House reports, it has "intensified its suppression of human rights . . . using arbitrary arrests and [its] onerous conscription system to control the population." Political prisoners languish in prison indefinitely. Privately owned newspapers are banned and "torture, arbitrary detentions, and political arrests are common."[35]

Laos (Lao People's Democratic Republic)

The scene of some of the most brutal fighting during the Vietnam War, Laos has mimicked Vietnam in trying to encourage foreign investment. But, as Freedom House reports, it is still a one-party dictatorship and "corruption and abuses by government officials are widespread. Official announcements and new laws aimed at curbing corruption are rarely enforced. Government regulation of virtually every facet of life provides corrupt officials with many opportunities to demand bribes."[36]

"Religious freedom is tightly constrained. The government forces Christians to renounce their faith, confiscates their property, and bars them from celebrating Christian holidays. The religious practice of the majority Buddhist population is [also] restricted. Gender-based discrimination and abuse are widespread. Poverty puts many women at greater risk of exploitation and abuse by the state and society at large, and an estimated 15,000 to 20,000 Laotian women and girls are trafficked each year for prostitution."[37]

North Korea (Democratic People's Republic of Korea)

The least free nation on earth, North Korea is tightening even further its control and repression of its citizens, according to Freedom House. Armed with nuclear weapons, North Korea is as isolated as ever. An hereditary dictatorship, power is handed down within to the progeny of founder Kim Il-sung. Freedom House reports that "protection of human rights remains nonexistent in practice. Corruption is believed to be endemic at all levels of the state and economy." The media is tightly censored and controlled and "nearly all forms of private communication are monitored by a huge network of informers." Things are so bad that even the UN General Assembly has recognized and condemned severe human rights violations, including the use of torture, public executions, extrajudicial and arbitrary detention, and forced labor; the absence of due process and the rule of law; death sentences for political offenses; and a large number of prison camps. The regime subjects thousands of political prisoners to brutal conditions, and collective or familial punishment for suspected dissent by an individual is a common practice.[38]

Saudi Arabia

Uniquely among the "worst of the worst" human rights abusers, Saudi Arabia is an American ally whose monarchy is sustained and kept in power by the US military. We import one million of the nine million barrels of oil the Saudis produce annually and Europe is even more dependent on the flow of fuel.

In our book *Screwed!*, we devote lots of space to documenting Saudi human rights abuses. Women are probably suppressed more here than in any other nation on earth . . . they may not legally drive cars, their use of public facilities is restricted when men are present, and they cannot travel within or outside of the country without a male relative. Daughters receive half the inheritance awarded to their brothers, and the testimony of one man is equal to that of two women in Sharia (Islamic law) courts.[39] What a wonderful country to have protected with the lives of our soldiers!

Somalia

Strategically located on Africa's eastern horn, Somalia has become a center for al Qaeda terrorists second only to the Afghan-Pakistan border.

Freedom House reports that "the political process is driven largely by clan loyalty. Due to mounting civil unrest and the breakdown of the state, corruption in Somalia is rampant. The office of the UN High Commissioner for Refugees estimated that there were 1.5 million internally displaced people . . . most of them living in appalling conditions."[40]

Sudan

This tormented nation is ruled by President Omar al-Bashir, for whom an arrest warrant was issued by the International Criminal Court (ICC) in March 2009, citing evidence of crimes against humanity and war crimes in Darfur. Meanwhile, the country is torn apart by tensions and war between Islamic Sudan and Southern Sudan, a new nation carved out from Sudan to protect the black minority from Arab terror. Behind the conflict is the oil-rich region of Abyei, mostly part of the north.

Freedom House reports that "the police and security forces practice arbitrary arrest, holding people at secret locations without access to lawyers or their relatives. Torture is prevalent. It is widely accepted that the government has directed and assisted the systematic killing of tens or even hundreds of thousands of people in Darfur since 2003, including through its support for militia groups that have terrorized civilians. Human rights groups have documented the widespread use of rape, the organized burning of villages, and the forced displacement of entire communities. Islamic law denies women equitable rights in marriage, inheritance, and divorce. Female genital mutilation is practiced throughout the country. The restrictions faced by women in Sudan were brought to international attention in 2009 by the case of journalist Lubna Hussein, who was arrested along with several other women for wearing trousers in public. They faced up to 40 lashes under the penal code for dressing indecently."[41]

Freedom House also lists Libya and Syria as among the "worst of the worst" but conditions in both nations are too unsettled to report reliably on their futures.

This litany of human rights abuses, governmental corruption, and suppression of democracy underscores our fundamental point: The United States should not surrender its sovereignty or decision-making power to a global body where these international miscreants are given full and equal voting power.

The world we face today is neither democratic nor honest. Neither respectful of human rights nor a guardian of individual liberty. It is dominated by corrupt dictators and one-party governments that do not speak for their people and keep power only by coercion, censorship, and repression.

We dare not trust our liberties to them.

CONCLUSION

SO WHAT DO WE DO ABOUT IT?

The treaties on gun control and the Law of the Sea are coming up for Senate ratification by the end of the year. President Obama and Hillary hope to ram them through the lame-duck session of the Senate after the elections have been held. In theory, they say they want to consider these documents without the pressures of election-year campaigning. But, in reality, they hope that defeated Democrats and retiring Republicans will give them the votes they need for ratification.

We must stop them!

Fortunately, the decision is in our hands. Democrats control only 53 votes in the Senate and 67 are needed to ratify a treaty. While the House doesn't get to vote on treaties, the two-thirds requirement in the Senate means that 14 of the 47 Republicans have to join with all the Democrats to get these treaties approved.

That's where we need to work. In our chapter on the Law of the Sea Treaty, we explain who are the swing votes. The nose count on the Arms Trade Treaty has not been taken yet, but it will likely follow the same pattern. Republicans who are not already opposed to the Law of the Sea Treaty are likely the ones whom we need to persuade to oppose the Arms Trade Treaty.

Because these Republicans are very, very sensitive to the opinions of their GOP backers back home, you can make a key difference. Contact them. Call their offices. Circulate petitions in your neighborhood and send them to their Senate offices. Get your local Republican clubs and other organizations to pass resolutions opposing ratification. Turn on the pressure.

Opposing the Code of Conduct for Outer Space Activities and preventing the president from signing on to the International Criminal Court will require broad public agitation. We need to publicize what these documents portend and what their implications are for the future.

We should be able to shoot down the Internet regulations. By arousing online users all over America, we can make it a dead letter even before it is signed. We need to kill it and we must!

Get to work!

In every generation, Americans have been called upon to fight to protect our liberties. Sometimes the threat came from an empire that ruled us. Then it arose from the invidious practice of slavery within our own borders. During the last century we were threatened by European and Japanese dictators who sought global domination. During the Cold War, we faced an ideological adversary who repressed human rights in the name of economic justice. In the War on Terror, we face an enemy that is determined to impose his religious and cultural values on us.

But the globalist adversary is more insidious and a greater threat to our liberty today than we face from any other source. It advances in the name of our own good, seeking to frighten us into line by dire predictions of global disaster unless we give up our sovereignty and share our wealth. Its apocalyptic predictions of environmental catastrophe come like tornado warnings on the prairie, leading us to come and huddle together in our shelters, accepting discipline and a loss of freedom during the emergency. But the emergency is fabricated and the warnings are issued just to panic us into the shelters, where we can be subjugated and tyrannized.

In his book *Ameritopia: The Unmaking of America*, Mark Levin writes how the desire for the elusive comforts of a utopia can induce men and women to surrender their personal liberty, accepting universal regimentation to achieve what they fantasize will be a greater good.

But fear can have the same effect. And those who would impose a global governance on us count on our worry about climate change, global warming, ocean acidification, rising sea levels, melting glaciers, and shifting rainfall patterns to get us into line behind a new world order.

But we are Americans and our knees don't bend to tyrants, however disguised.

ACKNOWLEDGMENTS

We are very grateful to Eileen's nephew and Dick's intern James McGann for his work in researching this book. A twenty-one-year-old with a great future! Clayton Liotta designed the cover. What great artwork! He is also the producer of our lunch alert videos and the illustrator of our Dubs books. Renaissance man!

Adam Bellow is our editor, and we love working with him and with all the people at HarperCollins. Special thanks to Kathryn Whitenight at Harper for her help.

Jim Dugan edited our manuscript and saved us from embarrassment and typo at every turn.

Thanks to Frank Gaffney at the Center for Security Policy for his advice and input.

NOTES

PART ONE

1. "fly-overs": Heather Johnson, "Feedlot Flyovers Draw Ire in Nebraska," *NP Telegraph,* June 2, 2012, http://www.nptelegraph.com/news/feedlot-flyovers-draw-ire-in-neb/article_55c22a61-4610-5c17-b8a5-5092454be7d0.html.
2. "chided critics": Nicole Gaouette, "Clinton Hits 'Black Helicopters' Crowd to Push Sea Treaty," Bloomberg News, May 24, 2012, http://www.bloomberg.com/news/2012-05-24/clinton-hits-black-helicopters-crowd-to-push-sea-treaty.html.
3. "This just in": Eric Pfanner, "Debunking Rumors of an Internet Takeover," nytimes.com, June 11, 2012, http://www.nytimes.com/2012/06/11/technology/debunking-rumors-of-an-internet-takeover.html?pagewanted=all/.
4. "Our global neighborhood": Commission on Global Governance, "Our Global Neighborhood," sovereignty.net, 1995, http://www.sovereignty.net/p/gov/gganalysis.htm.
5. "Acknowledging responsibility": Report of the Commission of Global Governance, "Our Global Neighborhood," gdrc.org, 1995, http://www.gdrc.org/u-gov/global-neighbourhood/chap7.htm.
6. "And as for": George Russell, "Exclusive: Godfather of Global Green Thinking Steps Out of Shadows at Rio+20," FoxNews.com, June 20, 2012, http://www.foxnews.com/world/2012/06/20/godfather-global-green-thinking-steps-out-shadows-at-rio-20/.
7. "Sovereignty has been": Commission on Global Governance, "Our Global Neighborhood," sovereignty.net, 1995, http://www.sovereignty.net/p/gov/gganalysis.htm.
8. "For the first": Marc Morano, "Flashback: Gore: U.S. Climate Bill Will Help Bring About 'Global Governance,'" climatedepot.com, July 10, 2009, http://climatedepot.com/a/1893/Gore-US-Climate-Bill-Will-Help-Bring-About-Global-Governance.
9. "will drive the": Bob Unruh, "Global Governance Coming With Carbon Tax, Says Gore," wnd.com, July 10, 2009, http://www.wnd.com/2009/07/103634/.
10. "individual states will": Joseph S. Nye Jr., "Global Governance," washingtonpost

.com, January 27, 2008, http://www.washingtonpost.com/wp-dyn/content/article/2008/01/24/AR2008012402329.html.

11. "the very idea": Jeffery Sachs, "Common Wealth," theglobalist.com, July 14, 2008, http://www.theglobalist.com/storyid.aspx?StoryId=7121.

12. "godfather": George Russell, "EXCLUSIVE: Godfather of Global Green Thinking Steps Out of Shadows at Rio+20," FoxNews.com, June 20, 2012, http://www.foxnews.com/world/2012/06/20/godfather-global-green-thinking-steps-out-shadows-at-rio-20/.

13. "developed and benefitted": Maurice Strong, *Stockholm to Rio: A Journey Down a Generation*, United Nations Conference on Environment and Development, 1992; quoted at http://sovereignty.net/p/sd/strong.html#8#8.

14. "Evidence procured": Claudia Roset, "The U.N.'s Man of Mystery: Is the godfather of the Kyoto treaty a public servant or a profiteer?," *Wall Street Journal*, October 11, 2008, http://online.wsj.com/article/SB122368007369524679.html.

15. "stepped aside": Warren Hoge, "Annan Failed to Curb Corruption in Iraq's Oil-for-Food Program, Investigators Report," *New York Times*, September 7, 2005.

16. "The concept of": Ibid.

17. "We have seen": F. A. Hayek, *The Road to Serfdom* (Chicago: University of Chicago Press, 2007), p. 166.

18. "What is called": Ibid.

19. "The movement for": Ibid.

20. The organization path: ABC News, abc.net.au, June 5, 2007, http://www.abc.net.au/news/2007-06-05/club-of-rome-member-warns-against-council/58734.

21. "an informal association": Club of Rome, clubofrome.org, http://www.clubofrome.org/?p=324.

22. "a common adversary": Ibid.

23. "either a real": Alexander King and Bertrand Schneider, *The First Global Revolution* (Hyderabad: Orient Longman, 1993), p. 85.

24. "In searching for": Ibid.

25. "For more than": David Rockefeller, *Memoirs* (New York: Random House, 2002), p. 405.

26. "Sacrilegious though this": Club of Rome, clubofrome.org, http://www.clubofrome.org/?p=324.

27. "deliberate disparagement of": F. A. Hayek, *The Road to Serfdom* (Chicago: University of Chicago Press, 2007), p. 155.

28. "our concepts of": Howard Green," "BNN Canada Interviews Maurice Strong," Maurice strong.net, http://www.mauricestrong.net/index.php/videos/141-bnn-canada-text-maurice-strong.

29. "[A] tax of $25": Michelle Nichols, "UN urges countries to impose global taxes to boos aid," Reuters, July 5, 2012, http://in.reuters.com/article/2012/07/05/entertainment-us-global-tax-un-idINBRE8640XP20120705.

30. "The prevailing unilateralism": Jeffery Sachs, "Common Wealth," theglobalist.com, July 14, 2008, http://www.theglobalist.com/storyid.aspx?StoryId=7121.

31. "Globalization, despite some": *Vatican Today,* news.va, October 24, 2011, http://www.news.va/en/news/full-text-note-on-financial-reform-from-the-pontif.

32. "citizen of the world": Barack Obama, Speech, Berlin, Germany, huffingontpost.com, July 24, 2008, http://www.huffingtonpost.com/2008/07/24/obama-in-berlin-video-of_n_114771.html.

33. "I speak as": Ibid.

34. "vaporous global-governance notion": David Brooks, "Loudly, With a Big Stick," nytimes.com, April 14, 2005, http://www.nytimes.com/2005/04/14/opinion/14brooks.html.

35. "We'll never": Ibid.

36. Email from Frank Gaffney to Dick Morris on July 1, 2012.

PART TWO

1. "cling to their guns": "Editorials: Democrats Cling to their Guns," Washington Times.com, October 27, 2011, http://www.washingtontimes.com/news/2011/oct/27/democrats-cling-to-their-guns/.

2. "I just want": "Obama: We're Working on Gun Control 'Under the Radar,' " FoxNews.com, May 25, 2011, http://nation.foxnews.com/guns/2011/05/25/obama-were-working-gun-control-under-radar.

3. "Reversed the policies": Sara Noble, "Small Arms Treaty of 2012—Elimination of the Second Amendment," independentsentinel.com, May 17, 2012, http://www.independentsentinel.com/2012/05/small-arms-treaty-of-2012-elimination-of-the-second-amendment/.

4. "governments must resist": "US joins Arms Trade Treaty talks, but at high price," Oxfam.org, October 15, 2009, http://www.oxfam.org/en/pressroom/pressrelease/2009-10-15/us-joins-arms-trade-treaty-talks-high-price.

5. "[S]mall arms are": "Small Arms," UN.org, http://www.un.org/disarmament/convarms/SALW/.

6. "But, in the": United States Crime Rates 1960–2010, disastercenter.com, http://www.disastercenter.com/crime/uscrime.htm.

7. "Of these": "Law enforcement, courts, prisons," census.gov, http://www.census.gov/prod/2011pubs/12statab/law.pdf.

8. US is the source of: Louis Charbonneau, "Arms trade treaty negotiations begin, Syria casts shadow," NewsDaily.com, July 2, 2012, http://www.newsdaily.com/stories/bre861077-us-arms-treaty/.

9. "We do not want": Ron DePasquale, "Talks Begin at UN on Global Arms Trade Treaty," ABCnews.go.com, July 3, 2012, http://abcnews.go.com/US/wireStory/talks-begin-global-arms-trade-treaty-16705286#.T_XnqRx-E3U.

10. "signed off on": Sara Noble, "Small Arms Treaty of 2012—Elimination of the Second Amendment," independentsentinel.com, May 17, 2012, http://www.independentsentinel.com/2012/05/small-arms-treaty-of-2012-elimination-of-the-second-amendment/.

11. "disguised as": Larry Bell, "U.N. Agreement Should Have All Gun Owners Up in Arms," forbes.com, June 7, 2011, http://www.forbes.com/sites/larrybell/2011/06/07/u-n-agreement-should-have-all-gun-owners-up-in-arms/.

12. "After the treaty": Sara Noble, "Small Arms Treaty of 2012—Elimination of the Second Amendment," independentsentinel.com, May 17, 2012, http://www.independentsentinel.com/2012/05/small-arms-treaty-of-2012-elimination-of-the-second-amendment/.

13. "The treaty is": Ibid.

14. "parties shall take": Maxim Lott, "Proposed U.N. Treaty to Regulate Global Firearms Trade Raising Concern for U.S. Gun Makers," FoxNews.com, August 5, 2011, http://www.foxnews.com/world/2011/08/05/proposed-un-treaty-to-regulate-global-firearms-trade-raising-concerns-for-us/.

15. "The UN's actions": Julian Pecquet, "Opposition to UN arms treaty heats up," thehill.com, July 2, 2012, http://thehill.com/blogs/global-affairs/un-treaties/235999-opposition-to-un-arms-trade-treaty-heats-up.

16. "Any international Arms": Chris Cox quoted in Julian Pecquet, "Opposition to UN arms treaty heats up," The Hill, July 2, 2012, http://thehill.com/blogs/global-affairs/un-treaties/235999-opposition-to-un-arms-trade-treaty-heats-up.

17. "on behalf of": NRA, "Beware Gun Owners, U.N. Moves Forward on Arms Trade Treaty," July 12, 2012, http://www.opposingviews.com/i/society/guns/nra-fights-second-amendment-un-moves-forward-arms-trade-treaty.

18. "Americans should realize": Ted R. Bromund, "The Risks the Arms Trade Treaty Poses to the Sovereignty of the United States," Heritage Foundation, June 4, 2012, http://thf_media.s3.amazonaws.com/2012/pdf/ib3622.pdf.

19. "This is a fantasy": Ibid.

20. "like the plague": Peter Brookes, "A Bad UN Idea on Arms Deals," nypost.com, July 1, 2012, http://www.nypost.com/p/news/opinion/opedcolumnists/bad_un_idea_on_arms_deals_7lTtoMqhmKFD2UnyGLf5qO.

21. "The treaty will": Ibid.

22. "[W]ho really expects": Ibid.

PART THREE

1. "thirty years ago, President Ronald Reagan": Donald Rumsfeld, "Why the U.N. Shouldn't Own the Seas," http://online.wsj.com/home-page, June 12, 2012, http://online.wsj.com/article/SB10001424052702303768104577460890850883780.html.

2. "What this treaty proposes is nothing": Ibid.

3. "But isn't that what": Ibid.

4. "no national interest": Dr. Harold Pease, "Treaty to Give the Oceans to the United Nations, Now Before the Senate," http://www.libertyunderfire.org/, June 11, 2012, http://www.libertyunderfire.org/2012/06/treaty-to-give-the-oceans-to-the-united-nations-now-before-the-senate/.

5. "The treaty's provisions were": Edwin Meese III, "Still lost on the Law of the Sea Treaty," http://www.latimes.com/, June 5, 2012, http://www.latimes.com/news/opinion/commentary/la-oe-meese-law-of-the-sea-20120605,0,6473043.story.

6. "the treaty would resurrect": Doug Bandow, "Cato Institute Foreign Policy Briefing No. 32: Faulty Repairs: The Law of the Sea Treaty is Still Unacceptable," Cato.org, September 12, 1994, http://www.cato.org/pubs/fpbriefs/fpb032.pdf.

7. "euphemistically called the": Ibid.

8. http://www.filmsite.org/night.html.

9. "no fight was more important": Doug Bandow, "Cato Institute Foreign Policy Briefing No. 32: Faulty Repairs: The Law of the Sea Treaty is Still Unacceptable," Cato.org, September 12, 1994, http://www.cato.org/pubs/fpbriefs/fpb032.pdf.

10. "may be worth": Senator Orrin Hatch and Senator John Cornyn, "The Law of the Sea treaty will sink America's economy," Foxnews.com, May 23, 2012, http://www.foxnews.com/opinion/2012/05/23/law-sea-treaty-will-sink-america-economy/.

11. "pursuant to the treaty's Article 82": Donald Rumsfeld, "Why the U.N. Shouldn't Own the Seas," http://online.wsj.com/home-page, June 12, 2012, http://online.wsj.com/article/SB10001424052702303768104577460890850883780.html.

12. "Over time": Ibid.

13. "This [treaty] would": Ibid.

14. "these sizable": Ibid.

15. "peoples who have": UNCLOS Part XI, Section 2, UN.org, http://www.un.org/Depts/los/convention_agreements/texts/unclos/part11-2.htm.

16. "Has more than": Dambisa Moyo, *Dead Aid: Why Aid Is Not Working and How There Is a Better Way for Africa* (New York: Farrar, Straus & Giroux, 2009), Introduction.

17. "In fact": Ibid.

18. "a kind of curse": Ibid.

19. "nations with mining": Senator Orrin Hatch and Senator John Cornyn, "The Law of the Sea treaty will sink America's economy," Foxnews.com, May 23, 2012, http://www.foxnews.com/opinion/2012/05/23/law-sea-treaty-will-sink-america-economy/.

20. "in other words": Ibid.

21. "if the enterprise": Law of the Sea Treaty, Un.org, http://www.un.org/Depts/los/convention_agreements/texts/agreement_part_xi/agreement_part_xi.htm.

22. "the Enterprise": Doug Bandow, "Cato Institute Foreign Policy Briefing No. 32: Faulty Repairs: The Law of the Sea Treaty is Still Unacceptable," Cato.org, September 12, 1994, http://www.cato.org/pubs/fpbriefs/fpb032.pdf.

23. "take measures": Ibid.

24. "as yet undetermined": Ibid.

25. "if any": Ibid.

26. "who would do": Ibid.

27. "all the more": Ibid.

28. "nations cannot": Ibid.

29. "why risk sacrificing": Edwin Meese III, "Still lost on the Law of the Sea Treaty," http://www.latimes.com/, June 5, 2012, http://www.latimes.com/news/opinion/commentary/la-oe-meese-law-of-the-sea-20120605,0,6473043.story.

30. "based in ideology": Matt Cover, "Hillary Clinton: Opposition to Sea Treaty Based on 'Mythology,'" cnsnews.com, May 23, 2012, http://cnsnews.com/news/article/hillary-clinton-opposition-sea-treaty-based-mythology.

31. "of course": Nicole Gaouette, "Clinton Hits 'Black Helicopters' Crowd To Push Sea Treaty," Bloomberg.com, May 24, 2012, http://www.bloomberg.com/news/2012-05-24/clinton-hits-black-helicopters-crowd-to-push-sea-treaty.html.

32. "proponents say": Senator Jim Inhofe, Senator Roger Wicker, and Senator Jeff Sessions, "Law of the Sea would usurp U.S. Navy's authority," politico.com, May 22, 2012, http://www.politico.com/news/stories/0512/76627_Page2.html.

33. "offering a new": Wayne Ma and James Hookway, "Vietnam Spars With China Over Oil Plans," wsj.com, June 27, 2012, http://online.wsj.com/article/SB10001424052702303649504577491823837421842.html.

34. "China, a LOST": Peter Brookes, "A pathetic pact for safety on the seas," nypost.com, May 22, 2012, http://www.nypost.com/p/news/opinion/opedcolumnists/pathetic_pact_for_safety_on_the_JRYvyyY47FPjx0pJOjzI0K.

35. "although Beijing ratified": Gordon G. Chang, "Should the US Ratify the UN Sea Treaty Because of China?," worldaffairsjournal.org, May 21, 2012, http://www.worldaffairsjournal.org/blog/gordon-g-chang/should-us-ratify-un-sea-treaty-because-china.

36. "supposedly need to": Peter Brookes, "A pathetic pact for safety on the seas," nypost.com, May 22, 2012, http://www.nypost.com/p/news/opinion/opedcolumnists/pathetic_pact_for_safety_on_the_JRYvyyY47FPjx0pJOjzI0K.

37. it is a lot: Frank Gaffney, "Common Sense on LOST," townhall.com, June 5, 2012, http://townhall.com/columnists/frankgaffney/2012/06/05/common_sense_on_lost/page/full/.

38. "by moving off": Gordon G. Chang, "Should the US Ratify the UN Sea Treaty Because of China?," worldaffairsjournal.org, May 21, 2012, http://www.worldaffairsjournal.org/blog/gordon-g-chang/should-us-ratify-un-sea-treaty-because-china.

39. "This is simply": Frank Gaffney, "Law of the Sea Treaty Is Wrong for US," newsmax.com, June 5, 2012, http://www.newsmax.com/FrankGaffney/Law-Sea-Treaty-Senate/2012/06/05/id/441292.

40. "In fact": Ibid.

41. "codifies navigational rights": Senator Jim Inhofe, Senator Roger Wicker, and Senator Jeff Sessions, "Hillary Tries To Neuter US Navy," foxnews.com, May 23, 2012, http://nation.foxnews.com/us-navy/2012/05/23/hillary-tries-neuter-us-navy.

42. "The most persuasive": Donald Rumsfeld, "Why the U.N. Shouldn't Own the Seas," http://online.wsj.com/home-page, June 12, 2012 http://online.wsj.com/article/SB10001424052702303768104577460890850883780.html.

43. "ceding any authority": Senator Jim Inhofe, Senator Roger Wicker, and Senator Jeff

Sessions, "Law of the Sea would usurp U.S. Navy's authority," politico.com, May 22, 2012, http://www.politico.com/news/stories/0512/76627_Page2.html.

44. "some fear the Navy": Ibid.

45. "could it be that": Ibid.

46. "outsourcing national security": Peter Brookes, "A pathetic pact for safety on the seas," nypost.com, May 22, 2012, http://www.nypost.com/p/news/opinion/oped columnists/pathetic_pact_for_safety_on_the_JRYvyyY47FPjx0pJOjzI0K.

47. "Does failure to ratify": Edwin Meese III, "Still lost on the Law of the Sea Treaty," http://www.latimes.com/, June 5, 2012, http://www.latimes.com/news/opinion/commentary/la-oe-meese-law-of-the-sea-20120605,0,6473043.story.

48. "Our ability to": Ibid.

49. "States shall adopt": David A. Ridenour, "Ratification of the Law of the Sea Treaty: A Not-So-Innocent Passage," nationalcenter.org, August 2006, http://www.national center.org/NPA542LawoftheSeaTreaty.html.

50. "look upstream": Sheril Kirshenbaum, "Sea Grant Fellows Forum," realoceans.word press.com, June 24, 2008, http://realoceans.wordpress.com/2008/06/page/3/.

51. Already, environmentalists have: David A. Ridenour, "Ratification of the Law of the Sea Treaty," www.nationalcenter.org, August 2006, http://www.nationalcenter.org/NPA542LawoftheSeaTreaty.html.

52. "LOST is a sweeping": Ibid.

53. "If Americans have": Michelle Malkin, "The push for the Law of the Sea Treaty," www.michellemalkin.com, October 2 2007, http://michellemalkin.com/2007/10/02/the-push-for-the-law-of-the-sea-treaty/.

54. "So why on earth": Ibid.

55. "the UN administered": Ibid.

56. "the predictable effect": Ibid.

57. "We are writing": Julian Pecquet, "Opposition to Law of the Sea Treaty heats up," www.thehill.com, May 25, 2012, http://thehill.com/blogs/global-affairs/un-treaties/229637-opposition-to-law-of-the-sea-treaty-heats-up.

58. "by its current": Ibid.

59. "To effect the": Ibid.

60. "If this treaty": Ibid.

61. Here's the list: Ibid.

PART FOUR

1. "has developed the": David Rohde, "China's New Export: Internet censorship," www.reuters.com, November 7, 2011, http://blogs.reuters.com/david-rohde/2011/11/17/chinas-newest-export-internet-censorship/.

2. "the Chinese model": Ibid.

3. "Putin commended": Josh Peterson, "Lawmakers move to reject proposals for U.N.

Internet regulation, www.dailycaller.com, May 31, 2012, http://test.dailycaller.com/2012/05/31/lawmakers-move-to-reject-proposals-for-u-n-internet-regulation/.

4. "if we are going": Patrick Goodenough, "Internet Regulation Returns to the International Agenda, www.cnsnews.com, May 29, 2012, http://cnsnews.com/news/article/internet-regulation-returns-international-agenda.

5. Touré, a native: "Hamadoun Touré," http://en.wikipedia.org/wiki/Hamadoun_Touré%C3%A9.

6. "while many US": Josh Peterson, "Lawmakers move to reject proposals for U.N. Internet regulation," www.dailycaller.com, May 31, 2012, http://test.dailycaller.com/2012/05/31/lawmakers-move-to-reject-proposals-for-u-n-internet-regulation/.

7. "could use the": Gordon Crovitz, "The U.N.'s Internet Power Grab," www.online.wsj.com, June 17, 2012, http://online.wsj.com/article/SB10001424052702303822204577470532859210296.html.

8. "It may be hard": Ibid.

9. "Brazil and India": Liza Porteus Viana, "US: New Battle Brewing At ITU Will 'Determine The Future Of The Internet," www.ip-watch.com, June 1, 2012, http://www.ip-watch.org/2012/06/01/us-new-battle-brewing-at-itu-will-determine-the-future-of-the-internet/.

10. "who are threatened": Ibid.

11. "the open Internet": Ibid.

12. "If all of us": Matthew Ingram, "Is the UN the next big threat to Internet freedom?," www.gigaom.com, May 31, 2012, http://gigaom.com/2012/05/31/is-the-un-the-next-big-threat-to-internet-freedom/.

13. "potentially dangerous": Liza Porteus Viana, "US: New Battle Brewing At ITU Will 'Determine The Future Of The Internet," www.ip-watch.com, June 1, 2012, http://www.ip-watch.org/2012/06/01/us-new-battle-brewing-at-itu-will-determine-the-future-of-the-internet/.

14. "having the UN": Nina Easton, "Where's the outcry on the U.N. push to regulate the Internet?," www.cnn.com, May 30, 2012, http://tech.fortune.cnn.com/2012/05/30/united-nations-internet-regulation/.

15. "to foster greater": Cale Guthrie Weissman, "Documents Leaked Detailing Proposals for UN Telecommunications Summit," www.opennet.net, June 21, 2012, http://opennet.net/blog/2012/06/documents-leaked-detailing-proposals-un-telecommunications-summit.

16. "these proposals show": Carl Franzen, "U.N. Proposals To Regulate Internet Are 'Troubling,' Leaked Documents Reveal," idealab.talkingpointsmemo.com, June 16, 2012, http://idealab.talkingpointsmemo.com/2012/06/un-proposals-to-regulate-internet-are-troubling-leaked-documents-reveal.php.

17. "the broadcast proposal": Ibid.

18. "would require member states": Ibid.

19. "other proposals": Ibid.

20. "[i]t must be": Congressional Cyber Security Caucus, http://congressionalcyber

securitycaucus.langevin.house.gov/index.shtml, http://congressionalcybersecurity caucus.langevin.house.gov/news/press-releases/2012/03/mccaul-langevin-lead -bipartisan-effort-to-prevent-international-internet-regulations.shtml.

21. "The principals stipulate": Sorcha Faal, "U.N. Move to Make Weapon of War Sparks Global Fears," http://www.envirosagainstwar.org/index.php, June 3, 2012, http:// www.envirosagainstwar.org/know/read.php?&itemid=12262.

22. "politely": "The U.N.'s Internet Power Grab," wsj.com, June 17, 2012, http://online .wsj.com/article/SB10001424052702303822204577470532859210296.html.

23. "both unnecessary": Ibid.

24. "weak responses": Ibid.

25. "Could limit": Doug Halonen, "House Takes First Steps to Block U.N. Regulation of Internet," yahoo.com, May 31, 2012, http://tv.yahoo.com/news/house-takes-first -steps-block-u-n-regulation-183411710.html.

26. "direct Internet": Ibid.

27. "Centralized control would": Lawrence Strickling, Philip Verveer, and Daniel Weitzner, "Ensuring an Open Internet," whitehouse.gov, May 2, 2012, http://www .whitehouse.gov/blog/2012/05/02/ensuring-open-internet.

28. "promote a global": Ibid.

29. "[t]his year, we're": Press Release, Bipartisan Leaders of the Committee Introduce Resolution to Preserve and Protect a Global Internet Free from Government Control, May 30, 2012, energycommerce.house.gov, http://energycommerce.house.gov/ news/PRArticle.aspx?NewsID=9554.

30. "If this power grab": Ibid.

31. "this resolution": Ibid.

32. "Does anyone here": Andrew Couts, "US gov't, Web titans go to battle against UN Internet power grab: Everything you need to know," digitaltrends.com, May 31, 2012, http://www.digitaltrends.com/web/us-govt-web-titans-go-to-battle-against-un -internet-power-grab-everything-you-need-to-know/.

33. "international regulatory intrusion": Press Release, Bipartisan Leaders of the Committee Introduce Resolution to Preserve and Protect a Global Internet Free from Government Control, May 30, 2012, energycommerce.house.gov, http://energycommerce .house.gov/news/PRArticle.aspx?NewsID=9554.

34. "I think a": John Peterson, "Lawmakers move to reject proposals for U.N. Internet Regulation," yahoo.com, May 31, 2012, http://news.yahoo.com/lawmakers-move -reject-proposals-u-n-internet-regulation-142206238.html.

35. "business leaders beyond": Nina Easton, "Where's the outcry on the U.N. push to regulate the Internet?," cnn.com, May 30, 2012, http://tech.fortune.cnn.com/2012/ 05/30/united-nations-internet-regulation/.

36. "swallow the Internet's": Associations, "A Battle for Internet Freedom as UN Meeting Nears," abc.com, June 22, 2012, http://abcnews.go.com/Technology/wireStory/ battle-internet-freedom-meeting-nears-16625777?page=3#.T_XnNmA2rKx .

PART FIVE

1. "green economy in": UNEP, "Toward a Green Economy—Pathways to Sustainable Development and Poverty Eradication," grida.no, 2011, http://www.grida.no/publications/green-economy/.
2. "world leaders and": Watts and Ford, "Rio+20 Earth Summit: campaigners decry final document," guardian.co.uk, June 22, 2012, http://www.guardian.co.uk/environment/2012/jun/23/rio-20-earth-summit-document.
3. "agreed that such": UNEP, "Toward a Green Economy—Pathways to Sustainable Development and Poverty Eradication," grida.no, 2011, http://www.grida.no/publications/green-economy/.
4. "decision supports": Ibid.
5. "decent employment and": UNEP, "Inclusive Green Economy Given Go Ahead by Heads of State at Rio+20," UNEP.org, June 2012, http://www.unep.org/Documents.Multilingual/Default.asp?DocumentID=2688&ArticleID=9195&l=en.
6. "reality that a": "Rio+20: Green Economy, SDGs, UNEP upgrade approved," *Daily Independent,* http://dailyindependentnig.com/2012/07/rio20-green-economy-sdgs-unep-upgrade-approved/.
7. "the Summit also": Ibid.
8. "mitigate the effects": Associated Press, "Clinton urges cooperation in resource-rich Arctic," usatoday.com, June 2, 2012, http://www.usatoday.com/news/world/story/2012-06-02/clinton-arctic-circle-cooperation/55344172/1.
9. "in climate aid": James Kanter, "A Pledge That Didn't Meet Its Potential," nytimes.com, November 27, 2011, http://www.nytimes.com/2011/11/28/business/global/28iht-RBOG-COP28.html.
10. "from its inception": Ibid.
11. "for people focused" Ibid.
12. "the administration of": Ibid.
13. "because wealthy countries": Jonathan Watts, "Rio+20 Earth summit: Walkout at 'green economy' talks," guardian.co.uk, June 14, 2012, http://www.guardian.co.uk/environment/2012/jun/15/rio-earth-summit-walkout-economy?newsfeed=true.
14. "amid a global": Ibid.
15. "We cannot be": Ibid.
16. "immune from legal": George Russell, "Mammoth new green climate fund wants United Nations–style diplomatic immunity, even though it's not part of the UN," foxnews.com, March 22, 2012, http://www.foxnews.com/world/2012/03/22/mammoth-new-green-climate-fund-wants-un-style-diplomatic-immunity-even-though/.
17. "possible conflicts of": George Russell, "U.N. Climate Organization Wants Immunities Against Charges of Conflict of Interest, Exceeding Mandate, Among Others," foxnews.com, June 12, 2012, http://www.foxnews.com/world/2012/06/12/un-climate-organization-wants-immunities-against-charges-conflict-interest/.

18. "lack of transparency": Ibid.
19. "the move to": Ibid.
20. "1.9 trillion per": James Helser, "Green Climate Fund Demands Diplomatic Immunity," thenewamerican.com, March 26, 2012, http://www.thenewamerican.com/tech/environment/item/7052-green-climate-funddemands-diplomatic-immunity.
21. "to use international": "Rio+20: Green Economy, SDGs, UNEP upgrade approved," *Daily Independent,* July 2, 2012, http://dailyindependentnig.com/2012/07/rio20-green-economy-sdgs-unep-upgrade-approved/.
22. "scaled-up and": George Russell, "The tab for U.N.'s Rio summit: Trillions per year in taxes, transfers and price hikes," foxnews.com, April 20, 2012, http://www.foxnews.com/world/2012/04/20/tab-for-uns-rio-summit-trillions-per-year-in-taxes-transfers-and-price-hikes/#ixzz1xzbVB8uS.
23. "Scaled-up": Ibid.
24. "there is currently": Felix Dodds and Michael Strauss, *Only One Earth: The Long Road via Rio to Sustainable Development* (London: Routledge, 2012), p. 169.
25. "help to clarify": Ibid.
26. "an estimated 25 percent": UNEP, "Inclusive Green Economy Given Go Ahead by Heads of State at Rio+20," UNEP.org, June 22, 2012, http://www.unep.org/GreenEconomy/InformationMaterials/News/PressRelease/tabid/4612/language/en-US/Default.aspx?DocumentId=2688&ArticleId=9195.
27. "pension funds to": Ibid.
28. "encourage governments to": Ibid.
29. "so few specifics": Mark McDonald, "U.N. Report from Rio on Environment a 'Suicide Note,'" nytimes.com, June 24, 2012, http://rendezvous.blogs.nytimes.com/2012/06/24/u-n-report-from-rio-on-environment-a-suicide-note/?emc=eta1.
30. "a failure of epic": Ibid.
31. "sophisticated UN": Ibid.
32. "affirm, recognize, underscore": Ibid.
33. "To be sure": Ibid.
34. "some of the": Bradley Brooks, "Rio+20, the unhappy environmental summit," AP/The Jakarta Post, June 23, 2012, http://www.thejakartapost.com/news/2012/06/23/rio20-unhappy-environmental-summit.html.
35. "[W]e saw anything": Ibid.

PART SIX

1. "After 12 years": AMICC, "Chronology of US Actions Related to the International Criminal Court," amicc.org, http://www.amicc.org/docs/US%20Chronology.pdf.
2. "the use of armed force": "Delivering on the promise of a fair, effective and independent court > than the crime of aggression," Iccnow.org, http://www,iccnow.org/?mod=aggression.
3. "Pressure [was] building": Reuters, "Bush Cancels Visit To Switzerland Due To Threat

Of Torture Prosecution, Rights Groups Say," huffingtonpost.com, May 25, 2011, http://www.huffingtonpost.com/2011/02/05/bush-switzerland-torture_n_819175.html.

4. "shall satisfy itself": Marion Smith, "An Inconvenient Founding: America's Principles Applied to the ICC," Heritage Foundation, February 18, 2010, http://www.heritage.org/research/reports/2010/02/an-inconvenient-founding-americas-principles-applied-to-the-icc.

5. "our government has": BBC News, "US to Resume Engagement with ICC," bbc.com, November 16, 2009, http://news.bbc.co.uk/2/hi/8363282.stm.

6. "so far completed": Eric Posner, "The Absurd International Criminal Court," wsj.com, June 12, 2012, http://online.wsj.com/article/SB10001424052702303753904577452122153205162.html.

7. "includes few authoritarian": Ibid.

8. "Now . . . it is": Ibid.

PART SEVEN

1. "orbital debris and": Rose Gottemoeller, "A Code for Outer Space, as Seen From the State Dept.," nytimes.com, March 15, 2012, http://www.nytimes.com/2012/03/16/opinion/a-code-for-outer-space-as-seen-from-the-state-dept.html.

2. "What the code would": Taylor Dinerman, "America's Suicidal Space Diplomacy," Gatestone Institute, January 12, 2012, http://www.gatestoneinstitute.org/2751/america-suicidal-space-diplomacy.

3. "Outer space has": John Bolton and John C. Yoo, "Hands off the Heavens," nytimes.com, March 8, 2012, http://www.nytimes.com/2012/03/09/opinion/hands-off-the-heavens.html.

4. "a transparent": Ibid.

5. "Obama is eroding": Ibid.

6. "term [is] often": Ibid.

7. "in a war": Ibid.

8. "if the United States": Ibid.

9. "the administration asserts": Michael Listner, "Congressional opposition to a Code of Conduct for space," thespacereview.com, February 6, 2012, http://www.thespacereview.com/article/2018/1.

10. "require the Department": Ibid.

11. "require the Department": Michael Listner, "Congressional opposition to a Code of Conduct for space," The Space Review, February 6, 2012, http://www.thespacereview.com/article/2018/1.

12. "Imagine": Email from Zubrin to Dick Morris, July 5, 2012.

13. "planetary protection": Ibid.

PART EIGHT

1. "'The European Union'": Elisabeth Rosenthal, "U.S. and Europe Battle Over Carbon Fees for Airlines," nytimes.com, July 27, 2011, http://www.nytimes.com/2011/07/28/business/energy-environment/us-air-carriers-brace-for-emissions-fees-in-europe.html?pagewanted=all.
2. "a group of": UN News Centre, "UN experts call for global financial tax to offset costs of economic crisis," UN.org, May 14, 2012, http://www.un.org/apps/news/story.asp?NewsID=41988&Cr=economic&Cr1=crisis.
3. "Where the world": Ibid.
4. "it is high": Ibid.

PART TEN

1. "97 smallest nations": Wikipedia, "List of Countries by population," http://en.wikipedia.org/wiki/List_of_countries_by_population#List.
2. All Told: "Voting Practices in the United Nations," 2010, www.state.gov, http://www.state.gov/documents/organization/162416.pdf.
3. In 2011, Freedom: Freedom House, "Combined Average Ratings—Independent Countries," 2011, http://www.freedomhouse.org/sites/default/files/inline_images/CombinedAverageRatings%28IndependentCountries%29FIW2011.pdf.
4. "A Partly Free": Freedom House, "Freedom in the World 2012: The Arab Uprisings and Their Global Repercussions," 2012, http://www.freedomhouse.org/sites/default/files/inline_images/FIW%202012%20Booklet—Final.pdf, p. 4.
5. Here's How Freedom: Freedom House, "Combined Average Ratings—Independent Countries," 2011, http://www.freedomhouse.org/sites/default/files/inline_images/CombinedAverageRatings%28IndependentCountries%29FIW2011.pdf.
6. "Corruption is the": "What is the Corruption Perceptions Index?," transparency.org, http://cpi.transparency.org/cpi2011/in_detail/.
7. They take a: Ibid.
8. "the perceived likelihood": Ibid.
9. They issue a: Ibid.
10. "series of in-country": Ibid.
11. "Here are the": "Demands for Better Government Must Be Heeded," transparency.org, http://cpi.transparency.org/cpi2011/results/.
12. The program included: Dick Morris and Eileen McGann, *Outrage* (New York: Harper Collins, 2007), p. 44.
13. "Corruption of the": "Probe: $1.8B diverted to Hussein regime," CNN.com, October 27, 2005, http://articles.cnn.com/2005-10-27/world/oil.food.report_1_oil-for-food-program-kickbacks-volcker?_s=PM:WORLD.
14. Paul Volcker estimated: Morris and McGann, *Outrage*, p. 59.
15. A year later: Ibid., p. 60.

16. "Un funding arrangements": Ibid., p. 64.
17. "As far as I am": Robert M. Appleton, "Chairman of the United Nations Procurement Task Force, to the United States House of Representatives, Committee on Foreign Affairs."
18. "the most disappointing": Ibid.
19. "The General Assembly's": "Internal Oversight and Procurement Controls and Processes Need Strengthening," GAO.gov, April 27, 2006, http://www.gao.gov/products/GAO-06-60IT.
20. "produce a document": George Russell, "U.N. Judges Charge Ban Ki-moon with Power Grab, Distortions of Their Rulings," FoxNews.com, November 11, 2011, http://www.foxnews.com/world/2011/11/11/un-judges-charge-ban-ki-moon-with-power-grab-distortions-their-rulings/.
21. "despite a net": Freedom House, "Freedom House Worst of the Worst," http://www.freedomhouse.org/sites/default/files/inline_images/Worst%20of%20the%20Worst%202010.pdf.
22. "His government . . . uses": Ibid.
23. "President Lukashenka systematically": Ibid.
24. "The State Peace": Ibid.
25. "The junta drastically": Ibid.
26. "has never": Ibid.
27. "The Chinese government": Ibid.
28. "Freedom of the": Ibid.
29. "is home to": Ibid.
30. "torture remains widespread": Ibid.
31. "one-fifth of all": Robert Zubrin, *Merchants of Despair: Radical Environmentalists, Criminal Pseudo-Scientists, and the Fatal Cult of Antihumanism* (New York: New Atlantic Books, 2012).
32. "Longtime President": Freedom House, "Freedom House Worst of the Worst," http://www.freedomhouse.org/sites/default/files/inline_images/Worst%20of%20the%20Worst%202010.pdf.
33. "of cannibalism, specifically,": Joshua Norman, "The World's Enduring Dictators: Teodoro Obiang Nguema Mbasogo, Equatorial Guinea," CBS News, May 22, 2011, http://www.cbsnews.com/8301-503543_162-20065072-503543.html
34. "has never held": "Freedom House Worst of the Worst."
35. "intensified its suppression": Ibid.
36. "corruption and abuses": Ibid.
37. "Religion freedom is": Ibid.
38. "protection of human": Ibid.
39. "the political process": Freedom House, "Freedom House Worst of the Worst." freedomhouse.org, http://www.freedomhouse.org/sites/default/files/inline_images/Worst%20of%20the%20Worst%202010.pdf.
40. "the police and": Ibid.

ABOUT THE AUTHORS

Dick Morris served as Bill Clinton's political consultant for twenty years. A regular political commentator on Fox News, he is the author of eleven *New York Times* bestsellers (all with Eileen McGann) and one *Washington Post* bestseller.

Eileen McGann is an attorney who, with her husband, Dick, writes columns for the *New York Post* and for their website, dickmorris.com. She has written extensively about the abuses of Congress and the need for reform.

DATE DUE